# PRESS B TO BELONG

# PRESS B TO BELONG

## Using Esports to Promote Inclusive School Communities

BY

**MATTHEW HARRISON**
*University of Melbourne, Australia*

**JESS ROWLINGS**
*University of Melbourne, Australia*

And

**DANIEL AIVALIOTIS-MARTINEZ**
*The FUSE Cup, Australia*

United Kingdom – North America – Japan – India
Malaysia – China

Emerald Publishing Limited
Emerald Publishing, Floor 5, Northspring, 21-23 Wellington Street, Leeds LS1 4DL

First edition 2024

Copyright © 2024 Matthew Harrison, Jess Rowlings and Daniel Aivaliotis-Martinez.
Published under exclusive licence by Emerald Publishing Limited.

**Reprints and permissions service**
Contact: www.copyright.com

No part of this book may be reproduced, stored in a retrieval system, transmitted in any form or by any means electronic, mechanical, photocopying, recording or otherwise without either the prior written permission of the publisher or a licence permitting restricted copying issued in the UK by The Copyright Licensing Agency and in the USA by The Copyright Clearance Center. Any opinions expressed in the chapters are those of the authors. Whilst Emerald makes every effort to ensure the quality and accuracy of its content, Emerald makes no representation implied or otherwise, as to the chapters' suitability and application and disclaims any warranties, express or implied, to their use.

**British Library Cataloguing in Publication Data**
A catalogue record for this book is available from the British Library

ISBN: 978-1-80455-927-7 (Print)
ISBN: 978-1-80455-926-0 (Online)
ISBN: 978-1-80455-928-4 (Epub)

INVESTOR IN PEOPLE

*This book is dedicated to the teachers and students in esports and to everyone who needs a safe space where they belong. You are the reason we get out of bed in the morning.*

# CONTENTS

| | |
|---|---|
| *List of Figures and Tables* | *xi* |
| *Foreword* | *xiii* |
| *Acknowledgement* | *xvii* |

| | | |
|---|---|---|
| 1. | Why Do Esports Present a Unique Opportunity for Building Inclusive Communities? | 1 |
| | Gaming and Esports: A Transcultural Wave | 1 |
| | Everyone Is Playing | 3 |
| | Not All Are Welcome | 5 |
| | School Systems Are Taking Notice of Esports | 6 |
| | A Case Study of One Country: School Esports in Australia | 7 |
| | What Is Being Taught Through Esports? | 8 |
| | How Did We End Up Researching Esports? | 9 |
| | Jess' Story: From Special Interest to Professional Pathway | 10 |
| | Matt's Story: Gaming for Connection | 11 |
| | Dan's Story: Gaming for Engagement | 12 |
| | Why Did We Write This Book? | 14 |
| | How Should I Use This Book? | 14 |
| 2. | Everyone Can Play | 17 |
| | What Is 'Inclusion', and What Does It Look Like in Our Schools? | 17 |
| | Addressing the 'Who': Labels of Identity and Differing Priorities | 18 |
| | Economic Disadvantage | 19 |
| | Gender Identity | 19 |
| | Neurological Differences | 20 |
| | Disability | 21 |
| | Ethnicity and Cultural Background | 22 |
| | Intersectionality Within School Communities | 23 |
| | Shifting the Conversation to Social Inclusion | 23 |

viii                                                                                              Contents

How Inclusive Are Our Schools? Exploring the Challenges          24
  Bullying in Schools                                            25
  Social Isolation                                               25
  Cultural Disconnect                                            26
Addressing the 'What': Creating a Framework for Inclusion in Esports   27
  Four Different Levels of Inclusion                             27
  Six Keys to Inclusion                                          29
    Key #1: Belonging                                            30
    Key #2: Interaction                                          31
    Key #3: Accessibility                                        31
    Key #4: Autonomy                                             32
    Key #5: Involvement                                          32
    Key #6: Acceptance                                           33
Addressing the 'How': Adapting These Frameworks to Our Esports
Communities                                                      33

3.  Creating Esports Programs That Overcome Socio-Economic
    Disadvantage                                                 37
Understanding the Challenges of Economic Inequality in Esports   38
    Games and More: Costs Involved With Esports Software         39
      Purchasing the Games                                       39
      Avoiding Microtransaction Madness                          39
      Broadcasting and Video-Editing Hardware
      and Software                                               40
    Big Gaming Rigs With Big Price Points                        41
    Managing the Cost of Staffing and Ongoing Professional
    Development                                                  42
    Creating Inviting Physical Esports Spaces on a Budget        43
    Taking the Show on the Road: Competition and Travel          44
Case Study: Mushroom Kingdom High School                         44
Everyone Can Play: Recommendations to Overcome Socio-Economic
Disadvantage in Your Esports Program                             47

4.  Breaking Down Gender Barriers                                51
Understanding Gender and Gaming Today                            52
    Historical Representations of Women in Gaming                53
    Challenging the Stereotypes of Female Gamers                 54
    Current Challenges Experienced by Female Gamers              56
    Systems of Support Empowering Female Gamers                  57
Case Study: Hyrule College                                       59
Everyone Can Play: Recommendations to Run an Esports Program
That Supports Female Players                                     61

Contents ix

5. Supporting Neurodivergent Players 65
   A Broad Umbrella of Neurodiversity 65
       Autism 66
       ADHD 67
       Dyslexia 68
       Other Conditions 68
   Gaming Communities as Spaces for Including Neurodivergent Players 69
       Challenges Experienced by Neurodivergent Players in
       Gaming Communities 71
   Case Study: Next Level Collaboration Gaming Group 72
   Everyone Can Play: Recommendations to Run a Neurodivergent-Inclusive
   Esports Program 75

6. Adapting Play for Diverse Physical Needs 79
   Finding Ways for Players With All Physical Abilities to Participate 80
       Gross and Fine Motor Needs 81
       Inclusion Is Voice and Choice: Empowering Player Agency
       When Selecting Hardware 82
       Types of Inputs That Can Be Used to Play Games 83
           Mouse and Keyboard Selection 83
           Adaptive Controllers 84
           Harnessing the Affordances of Touchscreens 85
           Motion Controls 86
       Adjustable Furniture 87
   Case Study: Sandover Special Development School 88
   Everyone Can Play: Recommendations for Including Players With
   Diverse Physical Needs 89

7. Celebrating Multiculturalism Through Esports 93
   Gaming as a Transcultural Phenomenon 94
   How Has Gaming Challenged Colonisation? 95
   What Is the Role of Community Around the Games We Play? 96
   Radicalisation Through Toxic Gaming Communities 98
   Play as a Force for Cultural Understanding and Harmony 99
   Case Study: Pallet Town Primary and Viridian City School 100
   Everyone Can Play: Recommendations for Celebrating
   Multiculturalism Through Esports 104

8. Supporting Regional, Rural and Remote Players 109
   Strategies to Minimise Geographical Isolation 111
       Bringing Students Together With School Serving as a
       Community Hub 111

| | |
|---|---|
| Mentoring Within the Community | 112 |
| Stronger Connections With Colleagues and Families Through Streaming | 114 |
| The Need for Online Professional Learning and Communities of Practice | 115 |
| Little Things That Can Make a Big Difference | 115 |
| Case Study: Zebes College | 117 |
| Everyone Can Play: Recommendations for Supporting Regional, Rural and Remote Esports Programs | 119 |

9. Taking the Next Steps in Establishing Your Inclusive Esports

| | |
|---|---|
| Program | 123 |
| Using Research to Address Concerns About School Esports | 125 |
| Talking About Violence in Some Games | 125 |
| Talking About Social Isolation and Gaming | 129 |
| Talking About Excessive Screen Time | 132 |
| Which System(s) Should You Purchase for Your Inclusive Esports Program? | 133 |
| Which Games Should You Be Playing in Your Inclusive Esports Program? | 133 |
| Rocket League | 135 |
| Pokémon Series | 136 |
| Just Dance Series | 137 |
| Mario Kart 8 Deluxe | 138 |
| Minecraft | 139 |
| Overwatch 2 | 140 |
| Gran Turismo 7 | 141 |
| League of Legends | 142 |
| Super Smash Bros. Ultimate | 143 |
| Hearthstone | 144 |
| Fortnite | 145 |
| Take a Minute to Remember Why We Became Educators | 146 |

| | |
|---|---|
| About the Authors | 149 |
| References | 151 |
| Index | 169 |

# LIST OF FIGURES AND TABLES

## Figures

| | | |
|---|---|---|
| Fig. 1. | Australian Gamers by Gender, Represented by Falling Blocks. | 4 |
| Fig. 2. | A Gamified Representation of Exclusion, Segregation, Integration and Inclusion. | 21 |
| Fig. 3. | Four Levels of Inclusion. | 29 |
| Fig. 4. | A Photo From the International Olympic Committee's Esports Trial in Singapore in 2023. | 38 |
| Fig. 5. | Female-Only Esports Tournaments in Traditionally Gendered Genres, Such as Fighting Games, Are Becoming More Popular. | 52 |
| Fig. 6. | A Next Level Collaboration Structured Gaming Group in Action. | 73 |
| Fig. 7. | Gamers With Physical Access Needs Are Gamers. | 80 |
| Fig. 8. | Mario Kart Competitions Have Become a Way for Students From Different Cultural Communities to Come Together Around a Shared Interest. | 101 |
| Fig. 9. | An Online Mentoring Program With Geographically Dispersed Players. | 113 |
| Fig. 10. | Shared Gaming Experiences Can Build Connections Between All School Community Members (Including School Pets). | 124 |

## Tables

| | | |
|---|---|---|
| Table 1. | The Everyone Can Play Inclusive Esports Framework. | 34 |
| Table 2. | Recommendations to Address Economic Inequality and Disadvantage in Your School Community. | 48 |
| Table 3. | Recommendations to Run an Esports Program That Supports Female Players. | 62 |
| Table 4. | Recommendations to Run a Neurodivergent-Inclusive Esports Program. | 76 |

| | | |
|---|---|---|
| Table 5. | Recommendations for Including Players With Diverse Physical Needs. | 90 |
| Table 6. | Recommendations for Celebrating Multiculturalism Through Esports. | 105 |
| Table 7. | Recommendations for Supporting Regional, Rural and Remote Esports Programs. | 120 |
| Table 8. | A Mapping of Game Rating Systems in Three Regions/ Countries. | 126 |
| Table 9. | Introducing the Most Popular Systems for School-Based Esports Programs. | 134 |

# FOREWORD

In introducing this book and its central themes, we are fortunate to have two transformative global leaders setting the scene in describing inclusive education and esports. Pasi Sahlberg is a Finnish education expert, renowned author and is currently a Professor at the University of Melbourne Faculty of Education. He has an established reputation as a global leader in education policy and innovation, having served as a Professor of practice at Harvard University and as the Director General at the Ministry of Education in Finland. Duane Mutu is the Founder and Director of Let's Play Live Media and an innovator in the New Zealand esports scene. He has long been a leading voice in expanding esports and ensuring that our gaming communities welcome all players. In introducing this book, Pasi and Duane bring differing but complementary emphasises on why school-based esports programs are so important in creating the conditions for a more inclusive society.

## The Need for Inclusion and Student Voice in Our Schools by Professor Pasi Sahlberg

As we delve deeper into the state of current educational institutions, two stark realities emerge. Firstly, as children progress in their journey from primary school to high school, their engagement in teaching and learning gradually wanes. Secondly, across the globe today, students' academic, social and emotional learning outcomes in school have declined. These sobering truths are not merely anecdotal; they are substantiated by empirical evidence and research. Studies reveal a concerning trend: students' motivation and engagement tend to dwindle from early childhood to adolescence. While primary school often serves as an engaging environment for children to explore the world and learn new skills, secondary school frequently sees the onset of boredom among teenagers.

Recent cross-national data paint a similarly bleak picture, indicating a decline in students' sense of belonging within schools over the past two decades. A sense of belonging encompasses the feeling of fitting in among peers, being accepted by the school community and having a meaningful role in the educational process. The repercussions of this diminishing sense of belonging are profound, manifesting in decreased attendance rates and heightened disengagement in school among students. Consequently, many schools are witnessing an erosion of vital qualities such as attention, curiosity, interest and passion among their students, ultimately resulting in a well-reported decline in academic achievement worldwide.

Addressing student disengagement and boredom presents a formidable challenge for today's education systems. While strategies such as aligning curricula with real-world relevance and fostering active learning methodologies hold promise, they may not suffice to cultivate a robust sense of belonging among all students. We need to do more than that. One potent approach to enhancing student attendance, engagement and learning lies in amplifying student voice and agency. Recognising that students should have a say in shaping their educational experiences, and empowering them to actively participate in decision-making processes that impact their schooling, can yield transformative outcomes. For example, in Australia, many education systems have recently added student voice and agency as key ideas in their education improvement agendas.

Schools that prioritise student engagement often undergo structural, procedural and cultural transformations tailored to meet their students' expectations and needs. Whether through interdisciplinary curricula, arts programs or innovative sporting initiatives, these schools understand that cultivating a compelling reason for students to attend is paramount to their educational success. Moreover, they recognise that when students are given the opportunity to pursue their passions within the school environment, their overall learning and growth flourish.

As the esteemed Sir Ken Robinson aptly remarked, 'Our education system has mined our minds in the way that we strip-mine the earth: for a particular commodity. And for the future, it won't serve us. We have to rethink the fundamental principles on which we're educating our children.' Sir Ken Robinson is right. Indeed, the future of education lies in nurturing students' innate curiosity, fostering creativity and encouraging them to pursue their passions. It is incumbent upon us to reimagine school education, placing emphasis on curiosity, creativity and passion for more inclusive and engaging schools. In doing so, we acknowledge the imperative to equip students not only with knowledge but also with the skills and mindset necessary to navigate an ever-evolving world.

## The Growth of Esports by Duane Mutu

In the dynamic landscape of contemporary culture and economics, few phenomena have ignited as swiftly and significantly as the meteoric rise of esports.

From niche pastime to global spectacle, the journey of esports has been nothing short of extraordinary. In this foreword, we embark on a journey to explore the profound cultural and economic impacts of this burgeoning industry, tracing its evolution over the past decade and examining the crucial role schools play in shaping its future.

The global cultural and economic impact of esports is nothing short of transformative. What once was perceived as a niche subculture has blossomed into a multi-billion-dollar industry, captivating audiences across the globe with its electrifying blend of competition, skill and entertainment. Esports tournaments now fill stadiums to capacity, drawing viewership numbers that rival traditional sports events. This seismic shift has not only redefined the concept of spectatorship but has also birthed a new generation of celebrities whose influence transcends traditional boundaries.

Over the past decade, esports has undergone a remarkable metamorphosis. From humble beginnings in the confines of basements and internet cafes, it has evolved into a global phenomenon with professional leagues, corporate sponsorships and mainstream recognition. Technological advancements have propelled the industry forward, enhancing the gaming experience and broadening its appeal to a diverse audience. Moreover, the emergence of streaming platforms has democratised access, allowing anyone with an internet connection to partake in the excitement.

Amidst this transformative landscape, the relationship between schools and esports has emerged as a pivotal force. Recognising the intrinsic connection between gaming and education, forward-thinking institutions have begun embracing esports as a valuable educational tool. By integrating esports into their curriculum, schools not only engage students in a field they are passionate about but also cultivate essential skills such as teamwork, communication and problem-solving. Moreover, esports provides a platform for students to explore potential career pathways in an industry ripe with opportunities.

As we navigate the complexities of the modern world, it becomes increasingly clear that esports is more than just a game – it is a cultural phenomenon with far-reaching implications. By understanding its cultural and economic significance, we gain insight into the transformative power of technology and its ability to shape the fabric of society. Moreover, by embracing esports as a tool for education, we empower the next generation to thrive in an ever-evolving digital landscape.

# ACKNOWLEDGEMENT

All illustrations are by Melissa Vallence.

# 1

# WHY DO ESPORTS PRESENT A UNIQUE OPPORTUNITY FOR BUILDING INCLUSIVE COMMUNITIES?

## GAMING AND ESPORTS: A TRANSCULTURAL WAVE

In reading this book, we assume that you have at least a cursory interest in gaming. If this is true, then you are not alone in this interest. Gaming has experienced exponential growth over the past five decades, becoming one of the most popular forms of entertainment worldwide. We are at a point in history where many of today's world leaders grew up playing arcade classics such as *Pac-Man* or owned an Atari 2600 or Nintendo Entertainment System (Adu, 2023; Grubb, 2017). With the advancement of technology, gaming has become more accessible, immersive and engaging, attracting millions of gamers from around the globe. According to a report by Newzoo (2024), a provider of market intelligence for the gaming industry, the global gaming market is expected to reach US$205.7 billion in revenue per year in 2026, which is almost four times the projected global revenue of the film industry for the same period (Statista Research Department, 2024).

When comparing these numbers, we can see the meteoric rise of gaming as a transcultural wave in most regions of the world (Palma-Ruiz et al., 2022). Some of the factors for this exponential growth include the proliferation of smartphones, the accessibility of freemium games (free to play, with the option of in-game purchases) and an explosion of online populations and online stores offering smaller game developers a viable platform to promote lower priced titles to a mass market (Kumar, 2021; Palma-Ruiz et al., 2022; Syahrivar et al., 2022). Smartphones have become more powerful, allowing gamers to play high-quality games on the go (Kumar, 2021). Cloud gaming, in theory, allows gamers to play games on any device without the need for high-end hardware, opening up gaming to a wider audience, although even Google has stumbled in making this a reality. As more people are playing games, the accompanying gaming culture has become part of mainstream society with streaming platforms like Twitch and YouTube making watching other people playing and talking about games almost as popular as actually playing games. Many a 12-year-old student can tell you all about PewDiePie, Ninja or Mr. Beast but would be lost when you asked them who won the Wimbledon tennis tournament in 2023 (Markéta Vondroušová won the women's final and Carlos Alcaraz won the men's final if you are scratching your head). PewDiePie alone has 111 million subscribers to his YouTube channel at the time of writing this sentence (PewDiePie, 2024). Perhaps this global popularity explains why other traditional modes of entertainment, such as professional sports organisations, have leaned so heavily into gaming culture. The Australian Open (another tennis grand slam) now broadcasts *Fortnite* battles (Australian Open, 2023), the English Premier League (football/soccer) has partnered with EA Sports to run a professional *EA SPORTS FC* league (Premier League, 2023) and the United States (US) National Basketball Association have likewise partnered with Take-Two Interactive to run a virtual basketball competition using the *NBA 2K* games (National Basketball Association, 2024). At the heart of these examples is the phenomena known as esports, or competitive video gaming, which is the focus of this book.

As gaming has exploded in popularity, it was only a matter of time before playing games became big business. According to a report by Statista (2023), the global esports market is expected to reach US$1.87 billion in revenue by 2025, up from US$194 million in 2014. If you are of a certain age and

---

### ⬇⬇⬆ CHEAT CODE: How can esports be defined?

Formosa et al. (2022) conducted a systematic review of definitions of esports and found that there is a lack of consensus around a common definition. From the numerous possibilities they shared, our preferred definition is the one used by the International Esports Federation because it is broad and highlights both the physical and mental dimensions required for participation:

*...a competitive sport where gamers use their physical and mental abilities to compete in various games in a virtual, electronic environment.*

*(Formosa et al., 2022, p. 10)*

remember watching the finale of the 1989 film 'The Wizard', you may also recall wishing that competitive gaming was as popular as depicted in that film. We now live in an age that far exceeds a mere theatre of people cheering on players' speed running through *Super Mario Bros. 3*. The only disappointment is that we are still largely using conventional controllers to play, rather than Power Gloves (although read Chapter 6 to keep the hope alive). Esports tournaments, such as the *League of Legends* World Championship and M5 World Championship, have become some of the most-watched events in the world, with millions of viewers tuning in to watch professional gamers compete for millions of dollars in prize money (Daniels, 2023).

## Everyone Is Playing

Historically, video games have been misconceived as an activity of interest to male children, teenagers and young adults. However, the rise of gaming as a global phenomenon has proven this stereotype untrue. We believe this misconception has, in turn, influenced popular perceptions of who would be interested in watching and participating in esports. The game development industry has continued to expand across a vast array of video game styles and genres, appealing to a wider range of demographics and audiences. According to the 2022 Digital Australia report, two-thirds of the Australian population plays video games, with the average age of gamers being 35 years (Brand & Jervis, 2021). Of those who play video games, 53% identified as male, 46% identified as female and 1% identified as gender diverse or non-binary, as shown in Fig. 1.

Shifting the focus to just teenagers, a Pew Research Center report found that a staggering 97% of teenage boys and 83% of teenage girls in the United States regularly play video games (Anderson & Jiang, 2018). These breakdowns might be surprising to many people, but if you work with children and young adults, you have probably noticed this shift over the past 20 years.

While console games have traditionally been associated with in-depth gameplay, the increasing prominence of tablets, smartphones and other handheld devices has given rise to mobile and other forms of 'casual' games. At times, this has created a point of tension within the gaming community as to who counts as a 'real' gamer. However, casual games have become increasingly popular and are often designed to be accessible to a wide range of players, with simple, easy-to-pick-up mechanics. This allows players to engage in shorter and more frequent play sessions, with the typical Australian casual gamer playing for 10 minutes twice a day (Brand & Jervis, 2021).

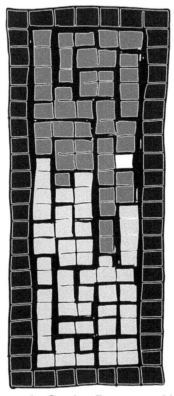

Fig. 1. Australian Gamers by Gender, Represented by Falling Blocks.

The increasing popularity of gaming has also brought attention to esports as an internationally represented competitive sport. Established in 2012, The International is an annual world championship for players of the multiplayer online battle arena game, *Dota2*, with prize pools totalling up to US$40 million (Michael, 2022). While such major league esports may focus on competitive success, esports at a smaller scale can provide benefits for a diverse range of players. When asked about their reasons for attending esports events, 42% of Australian gamers described a sense of belonging to a player community, and 41% enjoyed the social aspects of esports (Brand & Jervis, 2021). Only one in six respondents reported attending to become a better player, highlighting the value of esports in fostering a sense of community beyond the game itself.

## Not All Are Welcome

Despite the rapid growth of esports around the world, issues remain about who is welcome and who gets to feel safe participating in esports competitions. We are massive fans of Nintendo and their franchises, so we were so disappointed when we learnt about the relatively recent controversy in the *Super Smash Bros.* community. If you are not familiar, *Super Smash Bros.* is a popular fighting video game series developed by Nintendo. In 2020, allegations were made against several popular professional players. Without getting into the details, these included sexual misconduct and other forms of grossly inappropriate behaviour (Butler, 2020). As a result, a number of players were banned from participating in various *Super Smash Bros.* tournaments and events. These allegations led to widespread criticism of the *Super Smash Bros.* community, with many calling for greater accountability and a more proactive approach to preventing such incidents in the future (Walker, 2020). According to Walker, some female players also criticised the tournament organisers and other players for not taking allegations of sexual misconduct seriously enough and for prioritising the reputation of players and Nintendo over the safety and well-being of its members. As educators, we understand how important positive role models can be in the formative years, so throughout this book, we highlight positive examples while ensuring that we acknowledge the realities presented by some toxic communities.

While this controversy highlighted significant issues within esports, such as the lack of clear guidelines and protocols for addressing incidents of misconduct and the need for greater support and resources for victims of abuse, there have since been some positive developments. In response to the controversy, Nintendo belatedly released a statement condemning all forms of harassment and abuse and announced that they would be working with tournament organisers to establish new guidelines for online tournaments (BBC, 2020). Within the *Super Smash Bros.* community, organisations such as Smash Sisters and the Fête 1 and Fête 2 tournaments have taken steps to promote diversity and inclusivity around competitive play, including support for female players and the LGBTQI+ community (Greenway, 2023). These small but important steps have begun to repair the damage caused by the 2020 allegations.

Beyond the *Super Smash Bros.* esports community, other groups have been proactive in taking steps to address inappropriate behaviour and support diversity by creating safe spaces. A prominent example of self-advocacy in online gaming is *Autcraft,* a dedicated *Minecraft* server allowing autistic children to play together, with protections in place, to celebrate autistic identity while preventing harassment. *Autcraft* was established by Stuart

Duncan, a Canadian father who enjoyed playing *Minecraft* with his sons but found that autistic children (including one of his sons) were often bullied during online play (Thorbecke, 2017). Not only did these children experience in-game harassment, such as other players intentionally destroying their builds, but they were also subjected to verbal abuse and insults. In response, Stuart decided to create a safe space for these children where they could simply be themselves and was overwhelmed with interest from other families wanting to join what became the *Autcraft* server. This is a 'whitelist' server, meaning only approved players can join; players must submit an application to the administrators for review before access is granted (Rogers, n.d.).

---

### ▦ SIDE QUEST: Autcraft

*Autcraft* is a *Minecraft* server designed to provide a safe space for autistic players and allies. Interested players must apply to join, helping ensure this remains a safe space for the community.

🔗 https://www.autcraft.com

---

While the *Autcraft* server implements a range of additional measures to maintain a safe environment, unfortunately, 'trolls' still target and harass *Autcraft* players. This highlights the hostility that players can experience if they are perceived as different or belonging to a marginalised community (Duncan, 2016). We share some seminal research by Dr Kate Ringland into the impact of *Autcraft* on autistic players' sense of social connection and autistic pride in Chapter 9.

## SCHOOL SYSTEMS ARE TAKING NOTICE OF ESPORTS

Reflecting the shift in understanding, educators and school leaders are increasingly looking for ways to harness the cultural power of esports as a means for developing more inclusive and cohesive school communities. Following the global COVID-19 pandemic and associated lockdowns, the return to in-person schooling has seen a greater focus on creating communities where students feel like they belong. We know that the term 'belonging' is contested, especially in relation to school systems (for example, see Slee, 2019). So, we want to clearly articulate our definition as it features in the title and

Why Do Esports Present a Unique Opportunity 7

throughout this book. We are particularly interested in 'a sense of belonging' in relation to schools and other formal education settings where you might be establishing an esports program.

As this book is intended for a global audience, we have opted to use the OECD definition as we believe this will be the most familiar to educators around the world. We also feel that, as a starting point, it is largely inclusive of the labels of difference that we explore in this book. In discussing a sense of belonging in relation to esports, the emphasis on trust, acceptance, love and support resonates with us as educators and people with direct or family connections to people from historically marginalised communities. Our definition will continue to evolve as we work with and learn from young people and their advocates.

## A Case Study of One Country: School Esports in Australia

Globally, we have seen exponential growth of school esports leagues in the last 5 years, with schools and alternative educational programs incorporating esports into their curriculum and extracurricular activities (Reitman et al., 2018; Trotter et al., 2022; Zhong et al., 2022). What is particularly exciting is the imagination displayed by educators in establishing leagues specifically created to expand the pool of esports players. GameChanger Girls (and Allies) is a great example of this innovation in the Australian and New Zealand context, offering an esports program designed specifically for female and non-binary players aged 10–15 years, centred around the game *Minecraft* (Stuckey, 2022). Combining game design, science, technology, engineering and mathematics (STEM) education and tournament play, the program invites these students with an interest in gaming to form clubs and join a global community. It stands apart from traditional esports leagues by having the

---

**♦♦♠ CHEAT CODE: How do we define belonging in a school context?**

We use the definition adopted by the Organisation for Economic Co-operation and Development (OECD), which is based on the work of Baumeister and Leary (1995) and Maslow (1943):

*Sense of belonging is the need to form and maintain at least a minimum number of interpersonal relationships based on trust, acceptance, love and support.*

(OECD, 2019)

teams first design the games in *Minecraft* before they compete against other schools in tournaments using their own creations. The program comprises four championship areas: community engagement, game design, tournament champions and the 'Grand Champion' award. Founder Stuckey (2022) analysed data from the pilot, finding that participants expressed a strong desire to play games designed by their peers, connect with girl game designers worldwide and feel part of an inclusive community. This highlights the program's impact on fostering a sense of belonging and empowerment among young girls in the esports and game design spaces.

Another recent disruptor of school-based esports, partially responsible for growth in Australia, is The FUSE Cup. Founded in late 2019 in Australia by one of the authors of this book, The FUSE Cup has quickly evolved from its national roots into a global esports competition, connecting an international network of schools. Removing financial barriers to esports for school communities is a substantial focus of this program. Through offering three age divisions for students in Years 5 and 6 (typically 11 and 12 years old), 7 and 8 (typically 13 and 14 years old) and 9 and 10 (typically 15 and 16 years old), this competition bridges the transition from primary (elementary) and secondary schooling. It organises three competitions annually for each division, conducted both online and live, ensuring a supportive and social environment under the watchful eyes of educators. Competitions use non-violent, console-based games, chosen for their relatively low cost, ease of setup and minimal technical requirements (see Chapter 9 for a more detailed guide on inclusive hardware). The goal is to make esports accessible to every school in the country. Within the Australian division, competing schools are divided into regional sections within each state, promoting face-to-face competitions that culminate in state championship events. In 2023, over 50,000 players from 350 schools, across every Australian state, competed in The FUSE Cup, highlighting the giant steps this initiative has taken in a short time.

## What Is Being Taught Through Esports?

Not only do esports provide an interest-based mechanism to support inclusion, but they can also serve to teach other skills for life. The team-based nature of esports creates ideal conditions to practise collaborative teamwork skills, including strategies to create a positive and supportive group setting when working towards a common goal. Competitive team play also provides students with the opportunity to practise self-regulation skills during challenging or stressful situations, strategies to manage disappointment in a positive manner and overall resilience. In The FUSE Cup, skills to build healthy relationships with gaming are also integrated into the esports program to promote students' awareness of digital well-being and their capacity to balance gaming with other aspects of their lives. In a world where digital technology has become increasingly integrated into our lives, these skills are crucial to support overall wellness in our students' lives beyond school.

A systematic review by Zhong et al. (2022) revealed that different genres of esports games also have the potential to develop unique skills through their game design. Although much research focuses on the collaborative teamwork skills previously mentioned, studies have shown that the virtual 'society' in many massively multiplayer online role-playing games can encourage the development of broader life skills. These skills include project and time management, constructive communication, cultural understanding and occupational skills, including workplace literacies. Other genres, including real-time strategy (RTS) and multiplayer online battle arena (MOBA) games, require players to learn technical skills such as installing software, managing hardware and networks and troubleshooting (Zhong et al., 2022).

> ★ **RESEARCH POWER-UP:** The impact of esports participation on the development of 21st century skills in youth: A systematic review (Zhong et al., 2022)
>
> This review provides an overview of the research around esports and development of '21st century skills.' It includes a breakdown of the different skills young people have developed through participating in esports and which game genres have been shown to help promote certain skills. It also outlines some considerations for how esports can be incorporated into teaching practice and contribute to educational change.

## HOW DID WE END UP RESEARCHING ESPORTS?

All three authors of this book are educators who have used video games as tools and spaces for learning. But, it is our unique personal journeys that have helped us understand the potential of esports for developing a sense of belonging within our school communities. It is these lived experiences that drive our shared passion for removing the barriers for those who may feel on the margins of society.

## Jess' Story: From Special Interest to Professional Pathway

When I was 10 years old, my sister and I received a bright yellow box that contained a PlayStation 2 (PS2) and two controllers. It was the first of many consoles I've owned, and it still holds a place in my heart as one of my favourite gaming platforms. My sister and I generally had very different interests throughout our childhoods, but the PS2 was one thing neither of us could get enough of. We sank hours and hours into Sony's classic platform games, upgrading our comedically ridiculous weapons to the most extravagant form possible in *Ratchet and Clank* and getting our first taste of open-world exploration in *Jak and Daxter*. From there, our gaming repertoire became an ever-expanding list across all platforms and genres, thanks to regular loans of *Hyper* magazine from the local library, filled with game reviews, cheat codes and strategy guides. *Hyper* magazine is sadly no longer with us, but my sister and my love of platform games still stand strong to this day (along with all our original save files)!

For my sister and I, the PS2 not only provided a way to connect and build our relationship through our common love of games but also share knowledge and collaboratively approach challenging tasks. Like everyone, my sister and I have our own areas of strength; gaming created a way for us to celebrate each other's talents and support each other where we could. *Jak II* was renowned for being an excellent but particularly challenging game for its genre, and while some missions became frustrating after many failed attempts, having a second person to call in for support made it much more bearable. We soon realised that one of us could usually complete the mission much faster than the other and eventually worked out a system of delegation where the most brutal missions were simply left to whoever was the expert. Destroying cargo in the port was always my specialty, but to this day, I struggle to complete the Underport without calling in backup.

On a personal level, throughout my childhood, I knew I was different to the other children, but I never really understood why. My interests often didn't align with those of my peers, and I found it hard to build and maintain friendships. At times, this left me feeling like a PlayStation controller trying to connect with a room full of Xbox consoles. After I finished my schooling, I was diagnosed with autism and attention deficit hyperactivity disorder (ADHD), and I finally had an explanation for why I had always felt so different, but until that point, my love of games provided a point of connection between myself and my peers. I could have a conversation with classmates about what they were currently playing or offer them advice on a level they were stuck on. Although these exchanges generally didn't lead to ongoing

Why Do Esports Present a Unique Opportunity 11

friendship, our shared interest in gaming created opportunities for social interaction that I otherwise would not have had.

Throughout my career, I have had the privilege of working with many children to support their capacity in a range of skills; however, one client is particularly memorable. Like many teenage boys, he was not particularly enthused to be hanging out with a 20-something woman in speech pathology sessions. During one session, he mentioned his interests included the video game series *Dark Souls*, and I knew I had found a way to support his skill development that was meaningful to him. From that point, our session activities were designed to build from his encyclopaedic knowledge of *Dark Souls* and the vocabulary he had built around the games. Within weeks, not only had his skill development markedly improved but also his confidence at both school and home. At the end of our final session, he said that sessions 'had not been the worst thing ever', which I think counts as a success. I will admit, however, that despite his extensive guidance and advice, I am still terrible at *Dark Souls*.

It is these celebrations of strengths and moments of connection that have continually inspired my work as a speech pathologist, researcher and CEO and co-founder of Next Level Collaboration. For many of the children I have worked with, the value of celebrating their areas of strength and interest cannot be underestimated. Gaming is a passion for many young people, and building from this through esports can be an effective tool to support inclusion in the school setting. Whether we are a child or an adult, everyone wants to feel like they are valued. Inclusive esports are a powerful way to foster a sense of acceptance, support and belonging.

## Matt's Story: Gaming for Connection

As someone who completed a doctorate in the use of video games for promoting social connection, it might be surprising to learn that, as a child, I was never allowed to buy a Nintendo Entertainment System or Sega Master System. My brother and I were well aware of the existence of these systems, with my cousin having one that served as a powerful motivation to visit my grandmother's house where he was living at the time. Despite living in a console-less household, we did have a 286 computer and a bevy of games stored on 3.5-inch floppy disks, but these never quite measured up to the graphical prowess of *Super Mario Bros. 3* or the *Legend of Zelda*.

The other missing component was the lack of two controller inputs. This meant that multiplayer gaming involved taking turns using the keyboard rather than simultaneous play. At the time, my brother and I were envious of the affordances of two-player action on the Nintendo and Super Nintendo consoles, but this limitation actually presented some unintentional benefits. Sharing a single keyboard meant that we had to turn single-player games, such as the renowned classic *Commander Keen*, into ad hoc multiplayer experiences by sharing a keyboard. One player would use the directional keys to steer the protagonist through the 2D platforming environment, while the other player would oversee the jumping, pogoing (yes!) and shooting using combinations of the ALT and CTRL keys on our chunky grey IBM keyboard. To be effective in our respective roles, we had to communicate clearly, giving specific instructions, checking for understanding and then providing feedback to the other player. It wasn't always just my younger brother, as we used this system with visitors who would often call past our house. This system proved to be effective in transforming games designed for solitary play into inherently social experiences.

As I'd always seen gaming as a pro-social activity, I was caught off guard by the hesitancy of some of my teaching colleagues to bring games into our classrooms as a tool for teaching the skills I had developed through cooperative play. Early in my career, I began a lunchtime gaming club. Many teachers were supportive of this endeavour, but a number expressed reservations. They were concerned that children were already playing too many games (and this was before smartphones were common), and that they should instead be outside on the basketball court or kicking a football. To a certain extent, I understood their concerns, but for some of my students, lunchtimes were the most difficult part of the day. These students needed an environment that built on their interests and allowed them to feel safe before they could connect with their peers. My gaming club specifically targeted individuals who were frankly not welcome on the basketball court or football field. It is for these students that I believe esports is particularly powerful, as participation allows them to experience success and, most importantly, to feel like they have a valued place in their school community.

Dan's Story: Gaming for Engagement

I remember the day when my lifelong love affair began with both computers and gaming. I was in Year 3 when my school introduced me to the black and green pixel magic of an Apple 2E computer and a game called *Where in the World is Carmen Sandiego?* I was instantly hooked. I began volunteering to clean up the classroom, increased my dismal home reading frequency and agreed to pretty much any other task that would earn more time playing this new game. Even then, it seemed that digital technology had the power to engage and motivate learners.

Growing up in the western suburbs of Melbourne in the 1980s with first-generation European migrant parents, let's just say playing video games wasn't high on my parents' priority list. As a small business owner, my father used my longing for a gaming console as a way to help me understand the value of money and hard work. I would wash my parents' cars weekly and save my pocket money. My father challenged me to save half of the funds needed for my very own Atari 2600 (which cost an eye-watering AU$200) and he would put in the rest. What happened next surprised him and my whole family. I realised I needed to scale up my car washing business drastically and took to the neighbourhood every Saturday and Sunday morning with my bucket, sponge, soaps and tyre cleaner. Within two weekends, I'd saved over AU$150, much to the shock of my entire family.

Throughout my adolescent years, gaming was always a social activity. From playing epic full seasons of football (or soccer) on *FIFA* at my neighbour's house every Saturday afternoon with friends to all-night *Resident Evil* horror benders, gaming bought friends together. It's no surprise then that I found myself as an educator who specialised in introducing teachers and students to new technologies.

As an educator, I've always found it easy to connect with students and build a strong rapport. I've been able to weave in personal stories about my upbringing, my family and friends and share parts of my life with students, as well as use my love and knowledge of digital technology tools to create fun and engaging tasks. By doing so, students feel comfortable sharing aspects of their lives, their hobbies and their interests with me and the class. I would often use these interests to engage students and make curriculum and lessons relevant to what my students were interested in at the time. Maths concepts taught through Taylor Swift songs? Not a problem! Learning about character development and motivations by having students create direct messages (DMs) between Mario and Luigi? Absolutely. Creativity, technology and engagement were hallmarks of my teaching methodology. Working in schools, I found it odd that, despite the growing interest in gaming and esports, there were limited opportunities for students to compete at a school level. So, at the end of 2019, I bit the bullet, quit my secure teaching job and launched The FUSE Cup, and here we are in 2024 writing a book sharing my experiences.

## WHY DID WE WRITE THIS BOOK?

Over the past 10 years, we have personally watched and been a part of the rapid rise in school-based esports programs. As these programs have become more organised and as formalised leagues have been established, we have been increasingly asked and challenged about how we support a version of esports in schools that creates the conditions where everyone can participate and feel welcome. We have been amazed at the creativity, enthusiasm and perseverance of teachers, education support staff and parents who have often volunteered their lunchtimes and after school hours to run these programs. Likewise, the sheer joy of seeing students coming together and collaborating and competing at something meaningful to them puts smiles on our faces. As we shared earlier, all three of us have been personally impacted in positive ways by social gaming, so we feel a connection to the players we work with and their emotional journeys as they engage in esports.

Yet over the years, we also noticed patterns in who is playing and who is not playing. It is not a secret that the professional levels of esports are largely male-dominated affairs, yet the statistics about who is playing tell us this shouldn't be the case. We also have noticed that certain communities of players, such as those with physical disability, are rarely included in promotional materials for esports competitions or school leagues. In making these observations, we don't doubt the good intentions of teachers running esports competitions or school league organisers. Our experiences lead us to believe that one of the most fundamental barriers to more inclusive participation is knowledge around how to create more inclusive esports programs or competitions. This lack of attention extends to research priorities. While there has been some excellent research into inclusive gaming, this is still very much an emerging area of scholarship, so we have used non-academic grey literature, such as blogs and stories from the gaming press, and our own experiences to fill in the unknowns. And here we are, writing this book to offer anyone interested in esports the starting knowledge to open the door to more players in their communities and hopefully build a more inclusive world for all gamers.

## HOW SHOULD I USE THIS BOOK?

Think of this book as a buffet of knowledge and shared experiences. You can ground yourself by reading the first two chapters (the entrée if you embrace

Why Do Esports Present a Unique Opportunity 15

our loose metaphor) before launching into the main course, with each subsequent chapter focusing on a different lens for inclusion. We do suggest you read both this chapter in full (congratulations, you're almost finished with Chapter 1!) and Chapter 2, which introduces the central framework we use to explore the dimensions of inclusion. Following this, we encourage you to read the chapters in the order that makes the most sense to you, your interests and your context. Chapter 3 explores the challenges and possible solutions for setting up sustainable esports programs in schools serving communities experiencing socio-economic disadvantage. Chapter 4 focuses on breaking down gender barriers to participation and belonging in esports programs, while Chapter 5 addresses creating neuroinclusive experiences for players with differences such as autism and ADHD. In recent times, there have been exciting developments in inclusive gaming for players with physical disabilities, with Chapter 6 helping readers to navigate the world of alternative input devices for play. Esports communities offer unique opportunities to celebrate multiculturalism, and Chapter 7 provides ideas of how all schools can do this to ensure that everyone in the community feels welcome and celebrated. Chapter 8 speaks to the very real obstacles experienced by esports communities in regional, rural and remote communities. Finally, Chapter 9 provides practical guidance on how to harness all of this information, use the framework provided and engage with school leadership and the broader community to enact real change.

If you haven't guessed it by now, we are most definitively gaming nerds and fully embrace gaming culture. This reality is reflected in the naming conventions used in this book. To protect the identities of the teachers we interviewed as part of the research informing our guidance, we've replaced their actual names and the names of their institutions with pseudonyms based on gaming characters. Also, throughout this book (including this chapter), we've provided the following assists to help non-gamers and non-researchers understand the world of esports and research and to share complementary information we think you will find interesting.

---

**↓↓↑ CHEAT CODE**

Definitions or suggested wording that readers can use to explain concepts to colleagues or people unfamiliar with esports or inclusive education.

> **★ RESEARCH POWER-UP**
>
> We use these to point you to further reading about a topic or explore the underlying evidence.

> **⊞ SIDE QUEST**
>
> Esports can be fascinating, but we know that some people just want to get to the point. In order to avoid taking you on too many tangents, we have included these links to adjacent resources or articles that might be of interest to some but not all readers.

We recognise that it is not often in life that people get opportunities to do what they love as their profession. As you read this book, we hope that you sense our passion for esports and inclusive education, and that the stories shared by some truly exceptional leaders in the school esports community inspire you as they have inspired us.

# 2

## EVERYONE CAN PLAY

This chapter focuses on defining inclusion and better understanding the social needs of some marginalised populations that may be in your school. As incorporating research evidence becomes increasingly important to school systems around the world (Thomm et al., 2021), it is essential to present a research-informed analysis of social inclusion so that you can design an inclusive school-based esports program. While not always easy reading, we explore many of the challenges that the research tells us these communities face in seeking inclusion in their school.

Fortunately, change is just around the corner. Readers of this book will most likely be the change makers in supporting and advocating for young people on the margins of their school community. As esports is an emerging space, finding an existing scaffold for a school-based context can be challenging. To address this, we've adapted a well-established framework for promoting inclusion in our schools to fit the context of esports. In this process, we've synthesised our professional experiences and drawn on a wealth of academic research to emphasise the importance of player and community voice when planning and running an esports program. We call this the *Everyone Can Play Inclusive Esports Framework*.

### WHAT IS 'INCLUSION', AND WHAT DOES IT LOOK LIKE IN OUR SCHOOLS?

Following a period of outrage and a renewed social justice awakening in many Western countries, reconceptualising our communities to be more inclusive has become a priority for many educators. From the #MeToo movement raising issues around gender-based discrimination and violence to the series of tragedies leading to a resurgent Black Lives Matter movement, the last decade has reinvigorated community-based advocacy impacting both gaming culture (Cortez et al., 2022) and our school systems (Goldschmidt-Gjerløw & Trysnes, 2020). While these movements had their origins in the United States, they have resonated with marginalised communities around the world (Castejon et al., 2022; Horeck et al., 2023; Liao & Luqiu, 2022). Part of the solution to many of these societal challenges has been a renewed focus on school systems and curriculum as being agents of change, reconceptualising what we teach and how we teach to work towards a more inclusive future (see Chapman & Hobbel, 2022 for a further discussion of curriculum). For us as educators, this raises some important questions:

- Who exactly are we trying to better include in our society?

- What does inclusion mean to these diverse communities?

- How can teachers and schools change entrenched and complex social dynamics to promote inclusion and belonging?

It's important to acknowledge that this is a contested space, and there is no 'one-size-fits-all' answer to each of these questions. This chapter attempts to answer these questions in terms of the communities that we focus on throughout this book, but we're sure we've inadvertently excluded some voices. In reading this chapter, we hope that readers engage critically with our assumptions, and we welcome feedback on alternative perspectives.

## ADDRESSING THE 'WHO': LABELS OF IDENTITY AND DIFFERING PRIORITIES

As teachers and speech pathologists, we work regularly with young people who present with a wide range of 'labels of identity'. Some of these labels, such as economic disadvantage, are ascribed to these students by our education system. Others, such as 'neurodivergent' or 'Queer', are labels that challenge outdated societal norms and are often sources of individual pride. What these labels of identity all have in common is that they describe people who have been marginalised and, in many cases, continue to be socially excluded in our schools (see Chapman & Hobbel, 2022, for a comprehensive discussion of exclusion). This section provides an overview of how we understand some of the labels explored in this book and the implications for social inclusion within our schools.

Everyone Can Play 19

## Economic Disadvantage

Socio-economic status can be defined as people's access to material and social resources and their ability to participate in society (ABS, n.d.). It's been assumed for a long time that economic disadvantage can have a significant impact on social inclusion in schools (Cemalcilar, 2010; Yue, 2017), although Allen et al.'s (2022) analysis found that teacher support can increase all students' sense of school belonging, regardless of their relative socio-economic status. It will be no surprise to many educators that children from low-income families can face a range of barriers that limit their opportunities to participate fully in school life, with systematic inequalities often leading to intergenerational poverty (Mezzanotte, 2022; Zuo et al., 2023). Barriers may include financial constraints that prevent families from accessing extracurricular activities such as esports programs, lack of access to technology and resources and limited support for academic achievement (many of these are examined in Chapter 3). In relation to support for academic achievement, it's important to acknowledge that school is not a level playing field (Ainscow, 2020). Some families can afford private tuition, while others cannot. Some families can afford to have a parent with a high level of education not working to support their children, while for others, this is just not a reality. We argue that to promote social inclusion in schools, it is crucial to address the structural barriers that perpetuate socio-economic disadvantage through the resourcing of programs that are targeted to offer every student opportunities to engage in a broad range of experiences. School camps shouldn't only be available to wealthy school communities and neither should esports programs. A broad and equitably resourced school system will help ensure that all children have the opportunity to thrive academically, socially and emotionally, regardless of their economic background.

## Gender Identity

Historically, gender has been considered synonymous with biological sex. However, this definition has now shifted to consider gender a separate concept related to identity rather than biology. We now recognise that gender identity can exist outside the male/female binary, reflected in the non-binary, gender fluid and transgender communities (Suominen et al., 2021). While our understanding of gender identity has expanded throughout recent times, gender remains a key consideration in the context of inclusion and equity.

Students who identify as female or gender diverse are often less likely to receive the support they require within the school setting (Whitlock et al., 2020). This is particularly true for these students who are also part of other marginalised groups. Males who are neurodivergent or have additional learning needs are significantly more likely to be identified in childhood and, as a result, access appropriate supports (Whitlock et al., 2020). However, those who identify as female or gender diverse often present quite differently, and as a result, their support needs may not be identified until later in life (Lai & Szatmari, 2020).

Beyond the academic setting, gender identity also has potential implications in the context of social inclusion. Students who identify as non-binary or transgender may choose to express their gender identity through their physical appearance, which can attract social consequences such as bullying (Ferfolja & Ullman, 2021). When promoting inclusion and acceptance, it is imperative to consider how gender identity and diversity are supported across all dimensions of the school context.

## Neurological Differences

Neurodiversity refers to the natural variation in human brains and neurological differences that exist among individuals (Kapp et al., 2013; Rosqvist et al., 2020). It is a concept that recognises and celebrates the diversity of human minds, including different ways of thinking, processing information and experiencing the world. Examples of neurological differences include autism, dyslexia, attention deficit hyperactivity disorder (ADHD) and Tourette's syndrome, but it's important to remember that there may be many others in your school community.

Social inclusion is as essential for neurodivergent students as it is for their neurotypical peers; it can change their perception of whether school is a place for them (Education and Employment References Committee of the Australian Senate, 2023). Neurodivergent students are often disproportionately socially excluded in schools around the world. However, research shows that strength-based and neurodiversity-affirming supports can foster school environments that not only meet the needs of *all* students (Chen et al., 2021) but also reduce stigma and discrimination towards neurodivergence (McVilly et al., 2022). As educators, we see this play out every day, with the neurodiversity in our own lives bringing a richness of experiences to our schools and communities.

| | |
|---|---|
| **Exclusion** occurs when students are directly or indirectly prevented from or denied access to education in any form. | **Segregation** occurs when the education of students is provided in separate environments from other students, isolated from their peers. |

| | |
|---|---|
| **Integration** is a process of placing students with different labels in existing educational institutions as long as they can adjust to the standardised requirements. | **Inclusion** is a process of systematic reform with changes to content, teaching methods, structures and strategies with a vision serving all students with an equitable and participatory learning experience. We're all in this together! |

*Source:* Adapted from Hehir et al. (2016, p. 3).

**Fig. 2. A Gamified Representation of Exclusion, Segregation, Integration and Inclusion.**

## Disability

Before diving into a deeper discussion of supporting disabled students, we want to clarify that we use 'disability' as an umbrella term to include a broad range of functional needs. This includes those who experience challenges with fine and gross motor skills, are blind or have low vision, are deaf or hard of hearing or have an intellectual disability. However, whether a person identifies as disabled is highly subjective and often influenced by cultural and economic factors. It's important to remember that definitions of disability are likely to vary across different schools and countries. For example, being designated as having a disability in Italy requires a medical diagnosis, which excludes conditions such as dyslexia (Giulia et al., 2020). From our perspective, what really matters is that all people feel welcome and supported within our school communities regardless of the label used to describe their support needs.

Inclusive education is a universal human right. Building from the landmark Salamanca Statement 1994 (Framework for Action), the United Nations Convention on the Rights of Persons with Disabilities (United Nations, 2006) prioritises a universally inclusive system of schooling that promotes the rights and well-being of disabled people. Historically, opportunities for disabled children to build meaningful relationships with their non-disabled peers have been both deliberately and inadvertently discouraged through exclusion or segregation in schools or hospitals (Pfahl & Powell, 2011). Research shows that safe and inclusive education settings where disabled children have the same opportunities as their peers promote positive mental health and improve academic success for those children (Hehir et al., 2016; Jarvis et al., 2011). In Fig. 2, we've adapted Hehir et al.'s (2016) well-known visualisation of the differences between exclusion, segregation, integration and inclusion with a gaming twist.

## Ethnicity and Cultural Background

Race is attributed to individuals based on their physical features, whereas ethnicity encompasses a wider range of factors such as language, nationality, culture and religion (Bulatao & Anderson, 2004). Many schools have attempted to embrace multiculturalism at a local level by making efforts to create safe and inclusive learning environments that respect and celebrate diversity (Arneback & Jämte, 2022). One way of doing this is through decolonising our curriculums to promote the teaching and valuing of a wider range of knowledges and histories. Despite some fearmongering in the popular press, decolonisation is incorporating diverse cultural knowledges and experiences into the curriculum to challenge the Eurocentric bias that is often present in education (Arday et al., 2021). We explore these ideas further in Chapter 7 and offer some practical strategies for celebrating multiculturalism through your esports program. Through these efforts, we can aim to develop the cultural literacies of our students and help them gain a better understanding of the societies in which we live today.

## Intersectionality Within School Communities

The concept of intersectionality recognises that individuals can identify with multiple labels of identity, and this can have complex ramifications for planning to support these students. For example, Griffith (2023) reports on research suggesting that autistic people are more likely to be members of the LGBTQ+ community. It is important to remember that our students may experience multiple and intersecting forms of discrimination and oppression due to their social identities. This means that someone's experiences of schooling are not solely determined by one aspect of their identity but rather by the ways in which their multiple identities intersect (Nedera, 2023). For example, consider the case of a First Nations student who uses a wheelchair. They may experience direct and indirect discrimination due to the curriculum ignoring the histories and achievements of Indigenous peoples and also due to the physical inaccessibility of their campus. It is important to avoid making assumptions or relying on stereotypes about what a student may need based on their identities. Instead, teachers should take the time to learn about each student's unique experiences and understand them as individuals with their own interests, strengths and challenges.

## Shifting the Conversation to Social Inclusion

We recognise that many teachers, families and students view school as a place primarily for academic learning. While respecting this view, we argue that schools also serve a vital role in human development beyond discipline-based knowledge and skills. Focusing solely on high-quality teaching is not enough because it fails to realise the power of our school systems in shaping the world in which we live. Our schools are microcosms of broader society, and the views and values developed during this formative period are carried with us throughout our lives. To shift schools from places of social reproduction, where marginalised students become marginalised adults, to places of social change, we need to implement interventions and supports that aim to break down the barriers to social inclusion.

Supporting play in schools is one way to build social connections between students from different communities. Although play can take very different forms, it's a universal activity that all students can engage in, regardless of their cultural or socio-economic background (Gordon, 2008). By providing opportunities for inclusive play, such as establishing inclusive esports programs, we are solving one piece of this complex puzzle by creating conditions in which students from all backgrounds have the opportunity to interact and form meaningful connections. However, for these opportunities to lead to an ingrained change in culture that transcends your esports program, we need to think carefully about the challenges many students face in their daily experiences of school. Once we've identified these challenges, we can then plan to address barriers through strategically implementing multi-tiered systems of support (MTSS), hopefully including your esports program.

> ★ RESEARCH POWER-UP: Supporting students significantly behind in literacy and numeracy: A review of evidence-based approaches (de Bruin et al., 2023)
>
> How do you decide which students in your school receive support, and how do you know they require this support? Although focused on providing educational support and interventions to students in academic domains, this umbrella review provides an overview of the utility and underpinning evidence for the adoption of an MTSS framework in your school. We see value in such frameworks for schools planning, implementing and evaluating social capacity-building supports and interventions.

## HOW INCLUSIVE ARE OUR SCHOOLS? EXPLORING THE CHALLENGES

So, how inclusive are our schools? While we are based in Australia, this is a globally prominent question, and some commonalities transcend state and national borders. While local histories and social contexts distinguish education systems from each other, research presents a surprising number of commonalities that highlight the inherent humanity of the challenges faced by marginalised communities. Systematic conditions that enable bullying of these people, combined with a less deliberate but equally insidious sense of social isolation, are unfortunately transcultural experiences. Likewise, segregation on the basis of access to digital experiences and cultural marginalisation occurs in school communities around the world. Through naming these challenges, we hope to support you in identifying and beginning to address each of these as they manifest in your community. We will not pretend that esports completely solves these complex issues, but we do hope that creating an inclusive program within your school will at least provide a safe space for marginalised students.

Everyone Can Play 25

## Bullying in Schools

Bullying in schools at an individual level can be understood as repeated aggressive behaviour intended to cause harm, distress or discomfort to another person (Hellström et al., 2021). This can include physical, verbal or social abuse and can be perpetrated by an individual or a group. Even low-frequency instances of bullying can have long-lasting negative effects on the victim's mental and physical well-being (Armitage, 2021). Teachers and school support staff know that bullying is a significant issue around the world, with students from marginalised backgrounds often disproportionately affected by bullying (Able et al., 2015; Blake et al., 2016; Cook et al., 2016; Katz-Wise & Hyde, 2012). This deeply saddens us both as professionals who work with children and people with direct personal connections to experiences of bullying.

In our professional experiences, bullying, in most instances, is far more insidious than simply acts of direct physical violence. This observation aligns with a meta-analysis of 152 studies, which found that 80% of children with disabilities were not chosen as friends by non-disabled children due to factors such as social communication differences, externalising behaviours such as stimming and emotional dysregulation (McVilly et al., 2022). It's essential to pre-emptively create a safe and inclusive school environment that fosters social inclusion for all students, including those with disabilities. Educating students on the importance of empathy and understanding towards those who are different from them is key. Opportunities for inclusive play and social activities will help eliminate bullying and harassment of all kinds.

## Social Isolation

Social isolation can be defined as a lack of social connections or having few people to interact with on a regular basis and can be associated with feelings of loneliness (Australian Institute of Health and Welfare, 2021). Although a relationship between social isolation and loneliness may exist, loneliness exists as a separate concept defined by subjectivity. Specific definitions of loneliness vary; however, common themes involving emotional responses to an unmet human need for belonging exist across all perspectives (Heinrich & Guillone, 2006). Social isolation and loneliness during childhood are associated with an increased risk of developing mental health conditions such as depression and anxiety disorders, along with physical health conditions such as hypertension and diabetes that can persist into adulthood. Cognitive development may also be impacted by social isolation, which can affect children's ability to learn key skills for school engagement, such as reading and writing (Almeida et al., 2022).

Throughout the COVID-19 pandemic, the impacts of social isolation became a frequent topic of discussion. However, loneliness is something experienced by many students beyond the context of a global health crisis. As previously mentioned, children with disabilities or other differences are more likely to experience bullying or social exclusion by their peers and often have fewer reciprocal friendships (Able et al., 2015). These patterns present significant risk factors and highlight the importance of building inclusive settings that foster opportunities for social connection, thus supporting students' need to belong.

## Cultural Disconnect

Intersection and interaction between cultures are greater than ever in globalised societies. Many school communities are multicultural, with students coming from a wide range of cultural backgrounds, each possessing their own languages, traditions and social norms. Cultural disconnect, or cultural dissonance, reflects a mismatch between a person's own culturally based beliefs, values or behaviours and the sociocultural norms presented in their community (Martinez-Taboada et al., 2018). For students from culturally and linguistically diverse backgrounds, the school system is often structured around local cultural norms. In Australia and other countries within the Anglosphere, education is generally influenced by Western sociocultural norms, and students from diverse backgrounds are often expected to align with these standards within their schools. This is known as cultural assimilation, where a minority group adopts and conforms to the social and cultural norms of the majority group (Spielberger, 2004).

Historically, cultural assimilation has been enforced upon Indigenous peoples as a result of colonisation. In Australia, Aboriginal and Torres Strait Islander children were removed from their families from 1910 to 1970 and forced to assimilate into white culture. This not only led to intergenerational trauma for separated families but also significant loss of language and cultural identity, higher instances of mental health conditions and disadvantages accessing education (Common Ground, 2022). Similar practices of Indigenous cultural assimilation have also occurred in other countries that were colonised by European nations, including the United States and Canada, as well as those colonised by non-European imperialists, such as South Korea and Taiwan.

Understanding these experiences of cultural disconnect is integral to building inclusive school communities. While many students may not have directly experienced traumatic events such as separation, the effects of these historical practices can be passed down between generations. It's crucial to consider how the school setting can accommodate for and celebrate cultural diversity, along with the range of traditions and beliefs that shape identities in a multicultural community.

## ADDRESSING THE 'WHAT': CREATING A FRAMEWORK FOR INCLUSION IN ESPORTS

Teachers and school staff are, in many cases, in front of the research into creating inclusive esports programs, trialling and evaluating a wide range of strategies and supports to create a culture that welcomes players who might not always feel like they belong. There is a good chance that if you're reading this book, you have an interest in creating a more inclusive esports program in your school or setting and are looking for ways to transform this interest into tangible action. This final section of Chapter 2 introduces the *Everyone Can Play Inclusive Esports Framework*. We developed this framework by drawing on the conceptual thinking of Edström et al. (2022), who brought together Göransson and Nilholm's (2014) description of four levels of inclusion and Janson's (2005) Participation Model, which describes the key components required for inclusion (this was never published in English – thanks Google Translate!). While Edström et al. (2022) were interested in inclusion in schools, we've further expanded this thinking to focus specifically on the context of school esports.

## Four Different Levels of Inclusion

Gamers usually understand the concept of levels, progressing from an initial starting point towards a final challenge. Levels are a helpful way of knowing where you are in terms of completing the game, particularly when you have an overworld map showing your location in relation to your final destination. When considering the progress of your esports program in relation to inclusion, Göransson and Nilholm's (2014) work can provide you with a similar point of reference. In analysing 60 of the most cited research articles discussing inclusion, they looked for patterns and similarities in understanding inclusion, identifying four hierarchical levels. While it's important to note these authors were primarily interested in inclusion for students with disability, we found their descriptions to be flexible enough to consider inclusion from a much broader angle, encompassing diversity of gender, culture and socio-economic status. As is detailed later in this chapter, we've also expanded the examples provided to include specific illustrations shared by teachers facilitating esports programs.

Much like someone playing the timeless Nintendo classic *Super Mario Bros.*, inclusion begins at Level 1-1. As countless mouse pads, t-shirts and tattoos attest, there's nothing wrong with this first level; it's a starting point. At this initial level, referred to as Level A, inclusion involves the placement of a student in a mainstream esports program, which, as we explored earlier in this chapter, is commonly referred to as integration. However, placement with peers alone does not ensure inclusion. Inclusion requires addressing various factors such as teaching and coaching supports and strategies, accommodating diverse communication needs and creating an environment that values and respects differences. Being placed in a special or segregated class based on a characteristic does not qualify as inclusion, although we acknowledge that this is desirable in some instances. For example, some people who identify as First Nations players might want to have their own esports program to celebrate their cultural identity and to meet other people with a shared history and culture. Likewise, female players might want to start a Girls+ group to create a safe space with other gamers like them.

The second level of inclusive education, individualised support (Level B), goes beyond placement. Level B requires meeting the individual needs of players by providing bespoke social and coaching supports. This level focuses on the individual student's well-being and ability to develop their skills in the esports program. However, the exact methods of meeting social and skill needs can vary, depending on the context. The aim is to create a beneficial social environment for the student, where they feel included, secure and actively participating, engaging and discussing play.

But what if you could pre-emptively implement supports so that everyone feels included without the need for individual adjustments? While Göransson and Nilholm (2014) originally referred to Level C as 'general individualised', we prefer the language of 'universal support'. This focuses on putting in place supports and resources for all students in the esports program so that everyone can benefit from them. Level C requires drawing on the evidence of which supports and resources might be best placed to meet the social and skill needs of all players, considering the individuals in your group and their preferences and then offering the entire group a menu of options around how they participate in your esports programs. No one is singled out.

According to Göransson and Nilholm's (2014) framework, the fourth level of inclusion, Level D or 'community', goes beyond meeting the social and skill needs of all players. This final level emphasises the creation of communities in esports programs where diversity is valued and celebrated. As education professionals, creating community should be our esports goal. At this level, all players receive the necessary support to thrive socially and develop the skills to be successful. We agree with Edström et al. (2022, p. 7) that inclusive education is about 'listening to unfamiliar voices, empowering all members, and celebrating difference in dignified ways.' It is this emphasis on community and openness towards diversity that distinguishes Level D from Level C. While this may seem a little utopian in description, there are some concrete indicators of when an esports program has transcended universal support and a truly inclusive community has been established. Before exploring these indicators, Fig. 3 playfully summarises each of the four levels. These are referred to throughout the following chapters of this book.

Six Keys to Inclusion

To help you identify what all these levels might look like in your program, this section introduces the Participation Model, positioned by Edström et al. (2022) as a tool for identifying and supporting inclusive education at the

Source: Adapted from Edström et al. (2022, p. 5).

**Fig. 3. Four Levels of Inclusion.**

group level, rather than just focusing on children with disabilities. For teachers and school support staff looking to create inclusive esports programs for a range of marginalised students, including students with disability, this can be a great way to consider the necessary components for inclusion. The model outlines six aspects that, together, define the concept of participation in different cultures, with a focus on 'how' and 'where' social and academic inclusion takes place. As we're focused on gaming and esports, we refer to these as the six keys to participation, much like the keys required to unlock secret exits in *Super Mario World*. These are:

(1) belonging;

(2) interaction;

(3) accessibility;

(4) autonomy;

(5) involvement;

(6) acceptance.

While the model was originally presented as a way to categorise and understand the complex concept of participation, we argue that it can be effectively transported to the specific context of supporting all players in an esports program. Interestingly, Edström et al. (2022) presented their keys as continuums (from a concept being absent to being fully realised) but emphasised that students need to be offered all six aspects to achieve full participation. While we believe there is always more that can be done to improve inclusivity, spectrums are useful when developing an inclusive esports program, allowing you to consider the requirements against each key area.

### ⚷ Key #1: Belonging

When we step back and consider the defining characteristics of belonging, we find it useful to conceptualise both formal and informal aspects. Edström et al. (2022) defined formal belonging as the labels and groups to which a student belongs, such as being enrolled in a school or signed up to participate in an esports program. Informal belonging refers to the subjective feeling of being an important part of the group. Formal belonging is the most elementary category of participation, at the lower end of the participation spectrum. A student has to be allowed to join before they can feel they belong as a member of that group. Informal belonging is more subjective and can be difficult for teachers and school support staff to measure (Edström et al., 2022). However, to access full participation, both formal and informal belonging must be taken into account.

### 🔑 Key #2: Interaction

Interaction is described as the act of contributing to an activity with others, where each individual provides an important part of the whole. Drawing on the definition provided by Edström et al. (2022, p. 10), interaction involves 'the opportunity to be part of a community and to learn and develop through interaction with others' in school activities. Acceptance is crucial for students to interact fully. The absence of interaction in schools could be characterised by a lack of group or collaborative activities in class or lunchtime programs. Full interaction is marked by plenty of successful occurrences of cooperation and exchange between students. If you've ever seen team-based esports, you might have begun to understand the potential these programs offer and why we believe esports can be a vehicle for inclusion.

Creating inclusive spaces for interaction is not always easy. As described earlier in this chapter, there are a host of barriers that students experience within their school communities. Social anxiety may hinder students' willingness to interact with their peers, leading to social isolation. Cultural differences, such as customs and norms, may create misunderstandings that affect student interactions. Language barriers can lead to communication difficulties, particularly for non-native speakers. Lastly, bullying may negatively impact interactions, leading to a hostile environment that inhibits student participation in group activities. This book will help you navigate these challenges!

### 🔑 Key #3: Accessibility

Accessibility can be divided into three sub-aspects: physical, socio-communicative interaction and meaning context. Physical accessibility refers to the availability of the physical environment, while socio-communicative accessibility is the ability to understand and communicate with others. We felt that Edström et al.'s (2022) description of meaning context may be a little confusing, so we've renamed this category as 'Accessibility to interactions in meaningful contexts'. As suggested by our revised name, this involves understanding the meaning and purpose of what one is doing.

Sometimes, it's easier to understand a concept by considering what it is not. The absence of physical accessibility can be exemplified by a lack of necessary equipment, such as adaptive gaming controllers for people with physical disabilities. Unintelligible instructions and misunderstandings characterise socio-communicative inaccessibility for students with communication or language differences. Inaccessibility to meaningful contexts is exemplified by school activities that seem pointless to students, such as when a teacher fails to take into consideration the cultural knowledge of their students.

Full accessibility is only achieved when there is unimpeded access to the physical environment, social activities and all academic opportunities offered by schools. As you read this book, it is critical to consider these sub-aspects of accessibility (physical, communicative and cultural) and remember that all are important factors in creating a welcoming environment.

### 🔑 Key #4: Autonomy

At its core, autonomy refers to the ability to make decisions about one's own situation, including what to do, with whom and how to do it. Edström et al. (2022) described autonomy as the students' influence on teaching and their impact on their own learning. To achieve autonomy, accessibility to meaningful contexts is crucial. Authoritarian instruction with limited opportunities for student voice on form or content characterises an absence of autonomy. Full autonomy occurs when students have ongoing opportunities to influence the structure and content of an esports program and are well-informed about the full range of possibilities. Student agency is closely related to autonomy but is the capacity to take purposeful action and have a meaningful impact on one's own life or the lives of others. Students who have autonomy are more likely to feel empowered to take action and exercise their agency.

### 🔑 Key #5: Involvement

Student involvement refers to the degree of interest and joy that students feel towards an activity or task in school. As this is a subjective feeling that cannot be forced, it's challenging to measure from an external perspective. For example, a student may demonstrate involvement when asked to complete a project on volcanos if they are passionate about geology and find it interesting. Other students may simply not care about volcanos (gasp!) and not be involved. Student involvement can manifest in various ways in your esports program, such as through active participation in group discussions, completing optional training sessions or volunteering to orientate new players.

🔑 *Key #6: Acceptance*

Acceptance in school communities refers to feeling valued and respected by peers and teachers. It involves acknowledging differences and appreciating each other's unique strengths. We think most educators will agree that when students are accepted, they feel a sense of belonging, are more likely to participate in school activities and feel motivated to learn. Conversely, when students are rejected or bullied, they may feel excluded, anxious and demotivated. In the following chapters, we provide illustrations of how acceptance in an esports program can look, including celebrating diversity and creating the conditions for collaborative play between students from different walks of life. We need to remember that our modelling of acceptance as professionals will have a substantive impact on the culture of acceptance within our programs. As we like to say, culture is king (or queen).

## ADDRESSING THE 'HOW': ADAPTING THESE FRAMEWORKS TO OUR ESPORTS COMMUNITIES

After examining Göransson and Nilholm's (2014) four levels of inclusion and our six keys to inclusion, we can build from Edström et al.'s (2022) mapping and adapt their framework to define inclusion in esports communities. Rather than focusing on all aspects of school, we've created the *Everyone Can Play Inclusive Esports Framework* to provide education professionals with a way of thinking about each of the keys to inclusion at different levels in the specific context of school esports programs. Using this framework, shown in Table 1, you can review the example indicators to consider your esports program with a critical eye and identify at which level you are operating.

As you progress through the subsequent chapters, you'll explore a number of case studies of schools that have focused on improving one or more of the six keys to inclusion for a particular population of students. At the end of each chapter is a list of strategies for each of the six keys to help you implement change in your program and support these individuals through esports.

**Table 1. The Everyone Can Play Inclusive Esports Framework.**

| | | Example indicators of Level A | Example indicators of Level B | Example indicators of Level C | Example indicators of Level D |
|---|---|---|---|---|---|
| **Belonging** | Formal belonging | A teacher or teaching assistant brings a player to an esports program | Students with diverse needs can enrol in an esports program, but additional support may be required to help them fully participate | All students can enrol in an esports program and supports are available to help students with a range of needs fully participate | All students can enrol and fully participate in an esports program, and the program openly accepts and embraces the diversity of its enrolled members |
| | Informal belonging | | | All students in an esports program feel welcome, as if they are part of the group | All students feel secure and welcome in their esports program, that they belong to a player community that supports diversity and difference |
| **Interaction** | Opportunities to be a part of a community | | A student participates in group esports activities with support from a teacher or facilitator | When designing group activities, an esports program incorporates a range of strategies to accommodate all students' individual needs, preferences, and communication skills | When completing group activities, participants in an esports program demonstrate collaborative skills and consideration towards each others' needs |

| | | Example indicators of **Level A** | Example indicators of **Level B** | Example indicators of **Level C** | Example indicators of **Level D** |
|---|---|---|---|---|---|
| **Accessibility** | Physical accessibility | 🎮 A student with a physical disability attends sessions in an esports program | 🎮 A student with a physical disability works with an assistant to help them play games in their esports program | 🎮 An esports program plays games that align with the needs of all students participating in the program, including those with physical accessibility needs | 🎮 A school esports program plays a variety of games and provides hardware options to accommodate a diverse range of physical accessibility needs |
| | Accessibility to socio-communicative interactions | | 🎮 An individual student uses augmented communication to communicate with others in their esports program | 🎮 An esports program provides a range of communication options and strategies for all players who participate | 🎮 A school esports program plays a variety of games, and activities are structured to accommodate a diverse range of communication needs |
| | Accessibility to interactions in meaningful contexts | | | 🎮 Task information is provided using a range of communication strategies to ensure all players understand the purpose of activities in their esports program | 🎮 All participants understand the purpose of activities in an esports program, and players are supportive and accommodating of others' individual needs |

(Continued)

**Table 1.** (*Continued*)

| | Example indicators of **Level A** | Example indicators of **Level B** | Example indicators of **Level C** | Example indicators of **Level D** |
|---|---|---|---|---|
| • **Autonomy**<br>Opportunities to influence form and context | | | All students are given opportunities to make decisions in their esports program, and a range of strategies are provided to help them do so | All students are given a range of opportunities to make decisions in their esports program using various strategies that consider and support the diversity of its participants |
| • **Involvement**<br>Subjective experience | | | | Participants enjoy completing activities in their esports program, and demonstrate investment through active participation |
| • **Acceptance**<br>Being acknowledged and accepted by others | | | | Participants in an esports program recognise each others' differences, celebrate strengths, and are supportive towards areas of challenge |

# 3

# CREATING ESPORTS PROGRAMS THAT OVERCOME SOCIO-ECONOMIC DISADVANTAGE

When you think of esports, what images come to mind? Perhaps it's the bright lights of a professional gaming venue, players on a stage with large screens, arena-style seating and a dedicated commentary box. This is certainly the image projected by the popular and gaming media, with coverage of events like the International Olympic Committee's esports trial depicting a neon-drenched tech spectacle, as seen in Fig. 4.

A number of schools, colleges and universities in the United States have attempted to recreate this atmosphere, building dedicated spaces for hosting esports events in front of large crowds, complete with commentary booths and gift shops selling official team jerseys (Hennen, 2021). The appeal of such spaces in schools is obvious, recreating for students the atmosphere and excitement of what they've seen when watching professionals playing in high-stakes tournaments. Yet building and maintaining professional spaces is only within the reach of schools that can either afford to reallocate funds from other programs or receive donations from their community or sponsors. We strongly believe that esports should be financially accessible to every school community without the need for parents or caregivers to pay additional fees or for schools to be reliant on wealthy donors.

This chapter examines practical ways to mitigate the costs of esports software and hardware, strategies for managing the costs of staffing and professional learning about esports and advice on creating appealing physical environments for esports competitions on a limited budget. To illustrate these principles in action, we provide a case study of a school that has successfully established a program, on a minimal budget, working with young people in an

Fig. 4. A Photo From the International Olympic Committee's Esports Trial in Singapore in 2023.

economically disadvantaged community in Queensland, Australia. Through analysis of this case study and the research, we offer a series of recommendations for how schools and communities can circumnavigate some of the most commonly identified socio-economic barriers.

## UNDERSTANDING THE CHALLENGES OF ECONOMIC INEQUALITY IN ESPORTS

While we know that esports offer numerous tremendous benefits, such as fostering teamwork, strategic thinking and problem-solving skills (Canning & Betrus, 2017; Miller, 2021), we also need to recognise the pain points caused by financial constraints and understand how these can cause substantial barriers and insecurities (Gibson, 2021). Economic disadvantage significantly affects the viability and accessibility of esports programs in schools. Many schools struggle to invest in digital technologies hardware and lack stable internet connections. Students are disadvantaged in competition if they lack access to these resources at home and cannot practise in the same way as their

Socio-Economic Disadvantage                                              39

well-resourced peers (UNESCO, 2023; Warschauer & Matuchniak, 2010). In some schools, parents can help alleviate under-resourcing. Cho et al. (2019) highlighted the widening gap between wealthy families and low-income families in supporting schools to run interest-based learning activities. We've also observed that when it comes to esports competitions, participation fees, travel expenses and venue entry costs further limit opportunities for many students to engage in competitive gaming. Addressing these disparities is crucial to ensure that esports programs promote inclusivity and equal educational opportunities for all students.

## Games and More: Costs Involved With Esports Software

Purchasing and maintaining software for esports programs involves several costs that can strain tight school budgets, which rely entirely on limited government funding. These expenses extend beyond the initial acquisition of gaming titles and include ongoing subscription fees for some titles, software for broadcasting, as well as ensuring that gaming systems are receiving regular operating system updates to maintain compatibility.

### Purchasing the Games

One key expense that every esports program encounters is procuring the actual games. Esports often revolve around popular multiplayer titles, and acquiring licences for these games can be expensive. Popular competitive titles like *Super Smash Bros. Ultimate* or *Gran Turismo 7* require licences for each device where they are installed (Ready Esports, 2024a). For a classroom or lab setting, this can quickly add up, especially if a school aims to provide a variety of gaming experiences.

### Avoiding Microtransaction Madness

While some esports titles may be initially free to play, they often require the payment of microtransaction fees to access premium features or content. Popular titles like *Overwatch 2* necessitate payments to unlock skins or custom appearances for playable characters. While not required to play, this makes it very clear during competitions which schools can afford to purchase these optional extras and which simply cannot justify these additional expenses (Reza et al., 2022). While an inability to afford a custom skin can be disheartening for some players, the requirement of some 'free to play' games to purchase characters can be downright unfair. In games like *League of Legends*, individual characters need to be purchased (Ready Esports, 2024b). If you come from a school that cannot afford to purchase custom characters for every player, then you have a restricted roster and fewer options than otherwise possible. If your school does have the means to purchase additional characters, then your team can use their relative economic advantage to access more strategic options during play.

*Broadcasting and Video-Editing Hardware and Software*

As we explored in the introductory chapter, esports is more than just playing games. School-based programs often involve live-streaming matches or editing recorded gameplay footage for analysis and improvement. To do this, you need both hardware to capture video footage and software for streaming or editing that footage. The good news is that high-quality cameras are increasingly affordable, with options across a range of price points.

> 🎮 SIDE QUEST: The best camera for streaming in 2023: Webcams for going live on Twitch, YouTube (Tuting, 2023)
>
> This is a good summary of some popular choices for video cameras that are particularly well suited to streaming and includes a range of price points for different budgets.
>
> 🔗 https://www.oneesports.gg/gaming/best-camera-for-streaming-2023-live

Using specialised streaming software, such as OBS Studio or XSplit, and video editing tools like Final Cut Pro alongside multiple cameras adds a sense of quality to broadcasts or video replays. It allows students to develop professional broadcasting and video editing skills (White, 2020). Of course, quality usually costs more. While there are free or low-cost alternatives available, the professional-grade digital video tools that many students will have heard about through gaming forums and esports media require a substantial investment.

Socio-Economic Disadvantage                                     41

## Big Gaming Rigs With Big Price Points

Procuring high-end gaming PCs and latest generation consoles like the Play-Station 5 and Xbox Series X for school-based esports competitions is a significant financial endeavour, and it can be a difficult sell for enthusiastic teachers trying to convince their school leadership. These costs encompass both the initial investment in hardware and the ongoing need to keep the equipment up to date to remain competitive.

At the beginning of a school's esports journey, acquiring gaming PCs and latest generation consoles is often the most substantial expense (McAllister, 2019; Ready Esports, 2024a). Many students will tell you that these devices are essential for providing a high-quality gaming experience, with powerful processors, advanced graphics cards and ample memory. It's also important to keep in mind that the rapidly evolving nature of computer technology means that schools must allocate additional funds for maintaining and upgrading their hardware (see Jackson et al., 2011 for an interesting example in Namibia). Games become increasingly demanding on hardware as new titles are released, requiring schools to invest in regular upgrades to stay competitive. This recurring expenditure adds to the overall cost of running an esports program.

As the educators in the room, we need to understand where players' expectations of esports come from in order to explicitly discuss the role of branding and consumerism in the esports industry and, more generally, in most popular sports. Sponsorship of professional gaming competitions plays a pivotal role in shaping perceptions of what constitutes a 'real' esports competition, potentially placing undue pressure on schools to adopt the latest technology.

Nike and Under Armour sponsor professional US football players to create an association between high performance and their products. Similarly, gaming hardware companies will position their mechanical keyboards and mice as prerequisites to winning by paying professional gamers on Twitch to use their equipment exclusively (Freitas et al., 2020). Your students should understand that this is not just an act of wanting to encourage the growth of esports. These are strategic investments by these companies to promote the latest gaming hardware and titles, creating an expectation that 'real' esports competitions must exclusively feature cutting-edge technology and the newest games. This perception can pressure schools into believing that they must invest in the latest equipment to be taken seriously as esports competitors. We encourage schools to use refurbished hardware options or past-generation systems to reduce costs while still offering a competitive esports experience.

## Managing the Cost of Staffing and Ongoing Professional Development

Teachers know that the world of education is constantly evolving and, with it, the methods of engaging students in meaningful learning experiences. Like any school-based initiative, establishing and maintaining a school-based esports program requires an ongoing cultural and financial commitment to professional development for the teaching staff involved. Staff changes are commonplace in schools around the world but can disproportionally impact programs at schools experiencing financial insecurity (see Gibson, 2021, for an example). For programs to be sustainable, there can be significant costs in ensuring that the knowledge just doesn't sit with one individual who may end up leaving for another position.

We urge you to consider the following financial commitments in relation to initial professional development when introducing a new esports program:

- Developing a foundational knowledge of esports: we contend that program facilitators don't need to be experts in all things esports, but they require some knowledge of competitive gaming, game selection, the integration of esports into the curriculum and rules governing school esports leagues. Reitman et al. (2018) agreed, citing staff inexperience and unpreparedness as substantial risks to the reputation of a burgeoning school esports program. Not many schools would run a soccer or football program without a coach who understands, at the very least, the basics of the game, and this should be true for esports too. Training can come in the form of introductory after-school workshops, longer courses or ongoing peer coaching and mentoring. Depending on the options selected, the courses can quickly add up for schools with limited financial means.

- Upskilling school technicians to work with esports hardware: While school technicians likely received training in server maintenance and bulk installing software on personal computers, it is unlikely that they received training around setting up and maintaining dedicated gaming hardware. There is a history of administrators and school leaders expecting teachers to maintain and troubleshoot all digital technologies (Sandholtz & Reilly, 2004). Schools and regions need to invest in upskilling technicians through esports-focused training. This will ensure they feel part of the decision-making process and have the skills necessary to lift the burden of maintenance from the program facilitators.

Socio-Economic Disadvantage

- Joining professional associations: many educators find value in joining professional organisations that build networking opportunities and knowledge for esports program facilitators. While providing access to valuable resources and game developers shaping popular esports titles, professional associations also usually come with annual membership fees.

Professional development for educators plays a crucial role in the success of esports programs, ensuring that students receive a high-quality experience, with perceptions of 'quality' being particularly important at the outset of a new program to quell cynical voices in your community. By carefully considering and budgeting for these costs, schools can provide their students with a valuable and enriching esports experience.

## Creating Inviting Physical Esports Spaces on a Budget

As much as we all love a glow-in-the-dark wall graphic, we also know that such aesthetic touches will not ultimately herald the success or failure of your program. Creating a dedicated space for esports, often referred to as an arena, can be a significant expense. This includes outfitting the space with stations for holding screens and gaming hardware, comfortable seating and appropriate lighting and acoustics (Ready Esports, 2024a). Furthermore, maintaining this space will likely incur ongoing operational costs, such as ongoing power bills and internet connectivity. Functionality should always take precedence over flashy extravagance, so ask yourself: 'What is the minimum viable space I can curate to get my program started?'

For schools with limited budgets, there will be important strategic decisions to make. For example, investing in gaming hardware that can run games smoothly and at high resolutions is more critical than purchasing customisable keyboards with coloured keys or high-end gamer chairs. This is one reason we suggest beginning with console-based esports, as games will have been optimised for a single chipset used in these consoles. Reliable, high-speed internet connectivity, crucial for competitive play, should also be prioritised if your students are playing in online matches. Instead of splurging on branded merchandise or unnecessarily upscale furniture, schools can make more economical choices that still offer comfort and durability. Bring your own chair, we say! We believe that as an esports program matures within a school, students care more about team culture rather than the initial glitz and glamour of an elaborate arena.

## 44 Press B to Belong

### Taking the Show on the Road: Competition and Travel

Participation in competitive esports leagues can encompass travel costs and tournament fees, and these costs can accumulate rapidly. This is especially true when teams need to traverse great distances or even cross state lines to attend major events (SimStaff, 2022). Tournament fees, often necessary to cover venue and operational costs, can range from modest to arguably extortionate, especially for more prestigious competitions. For schools operating on tight budgets, these costs can be prohibitive, resulting in them either abstaining from participation or limiting the number of events they attend. This disparity can leave students in budget-restricted schools at a distinct disadvantage, not just in terms of competition but also in potential exposure to scouts or scholarship opportunities that can come from high-level tournaments. If you happen to also serve in a governance position within an esports organisation, we also encourage you to argue that leagues need to provide more egalitarian funding solutions and support structures to ensure every student, irrespective of their school's financial status, has equitable access to major tournaments.

### CASE STUDY: MUSHROOM KINGDOM HIGH SCHOOL

When talking about the students he works with at Mushroom Kingdom High School, teacher and esports program facilitator Luigi highlights the socio-economic challenges of the community but also the incredible resilience of the young people with whom he works. Of the 1,600 students, 42% of families are economically in the bottom quarter of Australia. Only 6% attending the school come from families located in the top quarter (we've deliberately not provided the reference for this data to protect the anonymity of the school). Luigi describes working with families in a region with historically high percentages of unemployment, with many of the participants in his esports programs coming from families who have experienced intergenerational unemployment and negative experiences of the education system. From an intersectionality lens, 47% of students speak English as an additional language with many students not speaking English in their homes. Luigi likes to think that his school has been developing a reputation as a caring place that supports students and their families in breaking intergenerational poverty through the use of innovative programs and pathways.

The esports program started in 2018 when Luigi was running a robotics and drone program; a reluctant participant asked if they could do esports instead. Luigi recognised that post-school pathways were a priority for a lot of students and their families, and he had recently read that esports was a billion-dollar industry, so he thought it worth investigating. After a successful pilot program, he ran his first full-year subject simply called 'Esports', which was mapped to the Australian Digital Technologies curriculum, but he also had content from five other areas of the curriculum. Initially, the school ran the program exclusively with Year 9 (typically 14 and 15-year-old students), as they were the most disengaged cohort within the school. As Luigi implemented this initial class, he collected data that showed a dramatic increase in attendance at school. Luigi and his colleagues have since expanded this program across all year levels. The programs have maintained a significant focus on school attendance and engagement for students from generationally unemployed families, seeking to make school a meaningful experience for students while communicating the importance of school to parents who had *not* had a great experience. Through a number of partnerships with higher education and industry, the program has also prioritised making possible careers in the games industry both visible and attainable.

A key part of the program's success has been inviting people outside the school to become part of the esports community. While the school serves students from Years 7 to 12, Luigi and a number of other staff have worked closely with feeder primary schools (those primary or elementary schools in the area that will most likely have their students attend this high school). Transition to high school can be daunting, so the esports staff wanted to build relationships with students before they graduated primary school and support teachers in these early years to run their own esports programs. This would keep these students excited about the possibilities of school. Luigi worked with these schools to co-author a curriculum. As more students began to dream about the possibilities beyond high school, Luigi also recognised that it was important to have a 'next step' beyond the completion of Year 12. He has worked with a university to write a Diploma of Esports. This provides a further professional pathway for his students, with a heavy emphasis on the application of the skills developed through esports into a range of careers related to digital technologies and services.

When asked about the specific supports he's put in place for his school's esports community, Luigi shared the structure he used, partially adapted from Harrison (2022). Creating a sense of predictability and safety by providing clear expectations of what will happen in each session is key to managing both excitement and anxiety. When developing and refining his esports class, Luigi was deliberate in teaching and practising routines, using a cyclical model of 'talk, reflect, empower, do'. The 'talking' is focused on dialogical instruction with the students in exploring the skills and strategies they will use during gameplay. In the 'reflect' stage, students are carefully guided through prompting to think about what they hope to achieve during that session of play. 'Empowering' helps students recognise how they can actualise their goals during the next session of play, with a focus on the teacher supporting them to understand the elements they need to practise. Finally, the 'do' stage involves 15 minutes of play. At the end of the 15 minutes, the students know it's time to return to the 'talk' stage, engaging in a subsequent discussion about what went well during play and where they need to focus their attention in the following session. The explicit teaching of such a system allows for a very orderly way of using gameplay as an opportunity for skill teaching and skill practice. Luigi notes that this structure also creates a sense of routine for his numerous neurodivergent students, with his school trying to create more inclusive spaces as they move away from a special education model towards fully inclusive classrooms.

Variety is also important for keeping students engaged. The school has a library of titles. Interestingly, they use the Australian independently developed classic, the *Untitled Goose Game*, for speed-running competitions. The *Just Dance* series and *Mario Kart 8 Deluxe* on the Nintendo Switch are most popular with the partner primary schools and Year 7 and 8 students. Trying to engage older students with school-appropriate games has been more challenging, but *Super Smash Bros. Ultimate* on the Nintendo Switch is a competitive hit with students from Year 9 to Year 12. First-person shooter games are a very popular genre, but they also make many teachers and parents uncomfortable. As a compromise with these older students, they can attend external competitions with the first-person shooter games *Valorant* and *Overwatch 2*, which are more focused on fantasy violence than realistic gun play. At one point, there was a big push from the students to play games in the *Rainbow Six* series, but Luigi put an end to this campaign because the series is simply too violent. Two of the most popular games for older students may come as a surprise. *Rocket League* and *Farming Simulator* have been very popular right across age groups, with teams from the school winning some state and national titles. Finally, the school has a dedicated group of students who compete in gamified Microsoft Office leagues. Yes, that Microsoft Office. You'll never look at Excel spreadsheets the same way again!

The school's esports program initially subsisted on modest donations of hardware and relied heavily on the generosity of the school's principal for staffing support. Recognising the need for a sustainable funding model, the teachers spearheading the program took a strategic approach to secure external sponsorship. They compiled and presented data demonstrating the positive impact of the esports program on student outcomes, including improved attendance rates and the development of employability skills, illustrating the value of the program to the broader community. By actively engaging local businesses and sharing their success stories through conferences and local news media, the school effectively communicated the mutual benefits of supporting the esports program. This concerted effort led to a remarkable achievement, securing \$34,000 a year in external sponsorship. For a school with a very tight budget, this financial boost not only ensured the program's sustainability but also highlighted the importance of community engagement and the power of showcasing real-world impacts to garner support.

## EVERYONE CAN PLAY: RECOMMENDATIONS TO OVERCOME SOCIO-ECONOMIC DISADVANTAGE IN YOUR ESPORTS PROGRAM

In Table 2, we bring together the research evidence and lived experiences to highlight examples of supports and strategies to address economic inequality and disadvantage in your school community.

**Table 2.** Recommendations to Address Economic Inequality and Disadvantage in Your School Community.

| Belonging | Accessibility |
| --- | --- |
| Formal belonging: | Physical accessibility: |
| • Find a source of funding, such as a sponsor, that enables for subsidised program and tournament fees for all players to ensure that cost is not a barrier for anyone<br>• Ensure that the program provides everything needed to participate with no additional purchases necessary | • Provide a range of controller options, chairs and other assistive technologies free of charge to students |
| Informal belonging: | Accessibility to socio-communicative interaction |
| • Provide team jerseys as part of being a member of the program, with the only cost being that players have attended three training sessions (you could hold a ceremony!)<br>• Insist that players should be using school-provided equipment to ensure that players don't feel left out by not having access to pro controllers or gaming laptops that their peers may own | • If you are running an online community for out of school training, use free software such as Discord but ensure this aligns with school and government policies |
| | Accessibility to interactions in meaningful contexts |
| | • Ensure that printed off newsletters and notices are available for every student to take home for those students who don't have internet access at home (or using cellular/mobile data is cost prohibitive) |

| Interaction | Autonomy |
|---|---|
| Opportunity to be a part of a community: | Full autonomy is where students have opportunities to influence form and context: |
| • Encourage enthusiastic players to come to your gaming space to practise rather than practising at home to include players who don't have access to hardware or software in their homes<br>• Begin by using free to play games that are available on lower cost devices in case players do want to practise outside of school hours | • Have a shared and transparent budget for your program and invite students to vote which games or hardware should be purchased using this budget, making it clear that this budget needs to include hardware and software for all of the players that are part of the community |
| **Involvement** | **Acceptance** |
| Subjective experience: | Being acknowledged and accepted by others: |
| • If scheduling training times after school, ensure that you have taken into consideration when public transport is easily available for your players to get home after training has finished | • Host school or sponsor-funded team lunches or dinners where caregivers and other siblings are invited to join, and alternate times to include families who have adults working night shifts |

# 4

# BREAKING DOWN GENDER BARRIERS

Historically, there has been a damaging stereotype that esports are largely designed for, or appeal to male students. This misconception stems from a long-standing assumption that only boys play video games, and girls or non-binary children have little interest. Traditionally, representations of women in video game media have been influenced by this assumption and depictions of female characters have often been problematic. While this remains in some cases, increasing attention has been brought to how women are portrayed in games, leading to a noticeable shift over the past decade. As industry and academic research has consistently shown that female players make up almost half of the gaming population, many companies have evolved to reflect this reality, not just in their portrayals of women but also in the communities surrounding their games. Moving away from gendering certain titles or genres of games, many companies have revised or implemented new systems to promote player safety in their online gaming communities. This includes female-only gaming competitions, as depicted in Fig. 5.

Although this has often been helpful in improving the experiences of non-male players, these changes have also led to backlash from gamers who disagree with how women are now portrayed and dislike the perceived restrictions on their online play experience. Gender-based toxicity in online spaces is still present. However, increasing attention has been drawn to its prevalence and research has shown that supportive environments can be a vehicle for changing attitudes around gender inclusion in gaming communities.

Fig. 5. Female-Only Esports Tournaments in Traditionally Gendered Genres, Such as Fighting Games, Are Becoming More Popular.

## UNDERSTANDING GENDER AND GAMING TODAY

Despite assumptions that gamers are primarily men and boys, research has shown that women make up almost half of Australia's adult gaming community. Of the 17 million Australian adults connected with video games, 46% identify as female (compared with 38% in 2005) and 1% identify as non-binary (Brand & Jervis, 2021). Data patterns show that, on average, female-identifying gamers in Australia spend 70 minutes per day playing video games. This figure is lower than for male players, who spend an average of 94 minutes per day engaged in gameplay (Brand & Jervis, 2021).

As the gaming industry has grown over time, the range of game genres, platforms and play style options has become increasingly diverse. While action, role-playing and combat-based games have remained consistently popular over time, simulation-based games have gained increasing prominence. These open-ended, creativity-focused games such as *Stardew Valley*, *Animal Crossing* and *The Sims* have often been marketed towards women, potentially due to their alignment with stereotyped associations between sociability, empathy and femininity. However, these games became especially popular throughout the COVID-19 pandemic and a new style of play emerged, dubbed 'cosy gaming'. Gamers from all demographics (including parents and older adults) found that the low-stakes, slow-paced nature of these titles evoked a sense of relaxation and 'cosiness' during unprecedented times. Cosy gaming has remained popular, highlighting a progressive shift away from gendered assumptions and an increasing focus on enjoyable, accessible gaming experiences for everyone.

## Historical Representations of Women in Gaming

Many video games have been developed with the assumption of a primarily male target audience and, as a result, female character designs have often intended to appeal to the male gaze. Women in video games have frequently been portrayed with unrealistic body proportions, hyper-feminine features and excessively sexualised, often impractical costumes. Their appeal has often been rooted in their visual aesthetic rather than their personalities, abilities or narratives. Many female characters serve as an accessory to a male protagonist or a plot device to facilitate his story, frequently falling into the trope of a 'damsel in distress'. Perhaps the most classic example of this is Princess Peach in the *Super Mario Bros.* series, in which she is frequently kidnapped by Bowser and, in some titles, forced into marriage. The player assumes the role of Mario, embarking on a journey across diverse worlds to rescue Peach from her fate. While Peach has become a playable character in several titles in the *Super Mario Bros.* series, she has only been the sole protagonist once in the 2005 Nintendo DS game *Super Princess Peach*.

Similarly, *The Legend of Zelda* series follows Link as he journeys around Hyrule to save Princess Zelda from Ganondorf's captivity. In earlier titles, Zelda was portrayed as relatively helpless despite her role leading Hyrule. However, her character underwent significant development in the 1998 release, *Ocarina of Time*. Central to the game's plot is Sheik, an androgynous, capable warrior who guides Link and teaches him skills. Sheik's background remains mysterious throughout the game until it is revealed that Zelda disguised herself as Sheik to help Link on his journey. While Link remains the protagonist in subsequent *The Legend of Zelda* titles, Zelda's character has become increasingly complex, with greater focus on her leadership as a ruler. This highlights a progressive shift in the representation of women in video games who are not just plot devices but fully formed characters with their own identities.

Perhaps one of the most culturally significant female characters in video game history is Samus Aran, the lead protagonist of the *Metroid* series. A skilled bounty hunter, Samus traverses the galaxy hunting space pirates in a powered exoskeleton. Samus' gender was initially ambiguous due to her full-body armour, and she was assumed to be male until the conclusion of the first game when she removed her helmet and revealed her identity as a woman. Although Samus' character is a strong, fearless woman, considered a break-through for leading female video game characters, she has remained subject to male-centric ideals. Players can unlock different endings in the *Metroid* series depending on their speed or percentage of game completion, each with Samus removing varying degrees of her suit.

Representation of women in video games has changed over the last decade, particularly in the physical diversity of women portrayed. *The Last of Us Part II* portrays Abby, a muscular, seasoned survivor of a zombie apocalypse who defies the delicate feminine appearance assigned to many female characters before her. Not only did Abby's character receive backlash and mockery from male gamers who disagreed with her appearance and strong physique, but this hostility was extended towards her voice actress. *Mass Effect Legendary Edition* edited certain camera angles from the original trilogy that involved female characters and were deemed gratuitous. While this decision was welcomed by many members of the gaming community, particularly women, other players expressed anger about the change and some even refused to purchase the game because of the edits. These examples illustrate that, despite progressive changes in the gaming world to create a more inclusive space for female players, women may not always be welcomed by other gamers.

> 🎮 **SIDE QUEST: The Last Us Part 2's Laura Bailey getting death threats over Abby role**
>
> This article describes the harassment Laura Bailey experienced as a result of her role playing Abby in *The Last of Us Part II*. It includes screenshots of abusive messages, including death threats that she received from fans who were unhappy with Abby's story in the game. The article has been updated with responses from the game's director and other industry professionals calling out the inappropriate behaviour and expressing support for Laura Bailey.
>
> 🔗 https://forbes.com/sites/paultassi/2020/07/05/the-last-us-part-2s-laura-bailey-getting-death-threats-over-abby-role/

## Challenging the Stereotypes of Female Gamers

Some of the major barriers to esports participation for female-identifying players stem from the long-standing stereotypes around female gamers' capabilities. There has been a long-standing stereotype that women are not as good at playing games compared to men. In many online multiplayer games, women who are highly skilled or achieve high scores are often accused of cheating, and women who engage in competitive gaming are often perceived to be overall less competent players. Their motives for playing might also be questioned, generally based on the assumption that they play to get attention rather than being genuinely interested in the game. However, these assumptions are rooted in sexism and research has shown that female gamers perform just as well as men do. Shen et al. (2016) found no significant disparity in performance between gender groups in massively multiplayer online (MMO) games, and female players progressed just as quickly as male players. When controlled for extraneous factors, findings indicated the perceived skill differences between genders are more likely related to confounding factors associated with gender (such as total play time or character class) rather than player gender itself (Shen et al., 2016).

★ **RESEARCH POWER-UP: Do men advance faster than women? Debunking the gender performance gap in two massively multiplayer online games (Shen et al., 2016)**

This study tackles some of the gendered stereotypes around gaming skills by analysing data from male and female players across two MMO games. It also raises some interesting points about gendered stereotypes and how they might exclude women from gaming.

With the rapid rise of smartphones, mobile and casual games have become increasingly popular. These games often have clear challenges and lower difficulty levels, which makes them appealing to audiences who may not have previously played traditional video games. While the accessible nature of these games can encourage participation from a range of demographics, some members of the gaming community have privileged traditional 'hardcore' video games and scorned casual games as 'inferior'. The presence of these attitudes has also reinforced a stereotype that casual games are enjoyed predominantly by female players, who are not interested in hardcore games as they are often more complex and challenging. As esports often include these hardcore games, the stereotypes around female players' preferences and their perceived inferiority can present a barrier to their participation in competitive play. While research has shown that gamers of all genders play both casual and hardcore titles, female players may be dismissed or considered less informed and less important compared to male players due to the gendered assumptions surrounding their gaming experience (Paaßen et al., 2016).

## Current Challenges Experienced by Female Gamers

Although the gaming landscape has undergone progressive changes in its representation and inclusion of women, female-identifying players still encounter unique challenges. They are more likely to experience discrimination and hostility during online play, particularly if it's easy for other players to identify their gender. It's not uncommon for players who use female-presenting or otherwise feminine avatars or whose voice or gamertag is likely to be perceived as feminine to be targeted by other players and subjected to gender-based harassment. As a result, female-identifying players often consciously choose gender-neutral gamertags and characters to avoid revealing their gender. Female-identifying players have also been known to use voice-changing software to sound more masculine when using voice chats in order to avoid sexism, while some players choose to avoid voice chat services altogether. An increasing number of platforms are employing additional measures to regulate player conduct, many of which involve consequences for inappropriate behaviour, including lifetime bans. However, community management guidelines generally operate in the context of individual games, leading to variability in these standards across the broader world of online play.

While esports are generally open to players of all genders, competitive leagues are historically male-dominated and often lack equivalent opportunities for female players. In competitive *FIFA* esports, female players may receive up to AU$2,800 initial investment to establish their team, compared to male players who often receive around AU$9,500 (Rose, 2023). Beyond initial financial investment, professional *FIFA* players who identify as female also receive comparatively less support through other forms of resourcing, such as coaching. In addition, many professional esports players rely on brand deals and online streaming to generate consistent income. While online streaming earnings are often similar for the top players regardless of gender, female-identifying players often have a smaller audience, which limits their opportunities for more lucrative brand deals and, in turn, their capacity to build a career from competitive play (Rose, 2023).

The traditionally male-dominated landscape of esports and the unique challenges experienced by female players can present a barrier to girls and women participating in competitive play. The comparative lack of opportunities presented to female players systemically disadvantages their representation in the esports space and, as such, their visibility as role models for girls and women who may be interested in esports. While the video game and esports industries have begun taking steps to support female players better, ongoing work is needed to continue addressing the challenges they currently face. Creating a truly inclusive space for girls and women requires meaningful change to break down systemic barriers and promote equal opportunities to players of all genders.

## Systems of Support Empowering Female Gamers

Morgenroth et al. (2020) found that more equal representation of female gamers could help reduce the traditionally masculine stereotypes associated with video games and promote inclusion in the gaming space. By presenting knowledgeable, skilled female players with diverse gaming interests, we can challenge the stereotype that female players are less competent and only play casual games (Yao et al., 2022). Research has also shown that upholding female-identifying players who defy the stereotypes associated with their gender can help reduce these perceptions (Yao et al., 2020) and increase positive attitudes towards female players (Yao & Rhodes, 2021). Rather than explaining the impacts of sexism, promoting female gamers as examples of competent players can be a more effective way to break down assumptions and reduce gender-based discrimination (Yao et al., 2022). By actively supporting and uplifting players who identify as female, we can create greater opportunities for girls and women to become visible role models that empower female players to participate in esports.

★ **RESEARCH POWER-UP: Gamer girl vs girl gamer: Stereotypical gamer traits increase men's play intention (Yao et al., 2022)**

This study investigates the relationship between male players' perceptions of female players and the extent to which they show stereotypical 'girl gamer' traits. Study results show that men expected more skill from women whose gaming profile demonstrated their competence and were more likely to play competitive video games with them than casual games. The authors highlight that, despite these findings, women are often not represented as competent gamers, and increasing the visibility of capable female gamers may present one strategy to help break down gendered stereotypes around gaming skills.

One strategy to increase the representation of female-identifying esports players is to consciously create space for them in esports teams and competitions. To address historical gender disparity, the F1 Esports Series has introduced a Women's Wildcard that guarantees a female racer a place in the F1 Esports Series Pro Exhibition. Here they can achieve a professional ranking and potentially be selected for an official esports team (F1 Esports Series, 2022). This initiative intends not only to increase the current representation of women in Formula 1 esports, but also incentivise more female players to participate in the future. An increasing number of esports leagues have also begun launching dedicated tournaments for female-identifying players to promote more inclusive play. The #GGFORALL initiative by prominent esports league ESL has set up ESL Impact, an all-women's *Counter-Strike: Global Offensive* (CS:GO) circuit that aims to increase diversity within the CS: GO community and create a safe environment for female players. The women's CS:GO circuit will also include a women-led council to promote female players' feedback to esports organisers. However, gender-specific tournaments such as ESL Impact have also received criticism for 'othering' female players and failing to address the underlying core issues presented by male players' perceptions of women in gaming.

Developing initiatives to specifically include female-identifying players is a first step to closing the gender gap, but these opportunities must be accompanied by sufficient resourcing to promote meaningful change. In the context of esports, female players should be provided with equitable support to their male counterparts, including coaching and management, along with financial investment for individual players, teams and winnings at competitive events. This can also build their capacity to participate in mixed-gender esports competitions, particularly in team-based games. Since 2021, leading esports organisation G2 has signed their first all-female esports teams to compete in mixed-gender *Valorant, League of Legends*, CS:GO and *Rocket League* tournaments. Members of the signed teams have praised G2 for providing equitable support and investment to female players and highlighted the value of representation for breaking stereotypes and encouraging girls and women to participate in esports. G2 has also emphasised their advocacy for diversity and inclusion through fostering talent regardless of gender and promoting role models to inspire the next generation of esports players (Gardner, 2023). By providing all players with an 'even ground', G2 has proven that female esports players are equally capable of success.

## SIDE QUEST: ESL #GGFORALL

ESL has set up a dedicated website with information on their #GGFORALL initiative, including the schedule for the all-female ESL Impact *CS:GO* circuit. The website also outlines the values underpinning the #GGFORALL project, including expectations for player conduct and partnering organisations working with ESL to promote safety and inclusion in esports.

🔗 https://esl.com/ggforall/

## CASE STUDY: HYRULE COLLEGE

Hyrule College is a combined non-government school in Queensland, with just over 1,350 students across Prep to Year 12. Overall, the students' families are from relatively advantaged socio-economic backgrounds, with 41% in the top quarter and 34% in the upper-middle quarter of Australia. Of the 1,350 students, 92% are from a native English background and 52% identify as female. When describing her school, esports leader and Head of Library Services, Zelda acknowledges the relative homogeneity of the student population and highlights her efforts to diversify representation in library resources. The school offers esports to students in Years 5–10 as part of the school's sporting program and an extracurricular activity. Zelda explains that esports programs run in multiple ways, with both competitive and non-competitive options, which has supported female student participation.

Zelda recalls her first interaction with The FUSE Cup in 2019 and the value of structured support and step-by-step guidance. Having access to established behavioural guidelines and resources on digital safety and healthy gaming habits provided Zelda with a strong foundation to gain leadership support for the esports program. She recounts some challenges in starting the esports program, particularly having to transition quickly to online play in response to the COVID-19 pandemic. The online setting felt more isolated with reduced social focus, and students didn't seem fully engaged compared to dynamic and fun live events. It was at a live The FUSE Cup event that Zelda learnt of an esports competition exclusively for female-identifying players, which received an 'ecstatic' response from her female-identifying players.

Many of Zelda's female-identifying players were happy to play in mixed competitions, but the exclusively female esports competition was 'a space for us, and only us' that felt safer. Zelda explains how this safe space not only supports friendship and a sense of belonging, but has also encouraged more female-identifying students to join the esports program (including those who might not usually be interested in gaming). She also describes a culture among her female esports community of 'girls supporting girls'. In one instance, she witnessed players from other teams rallying around an upset player to offer her comfort after losing a game at a competition event. Zelda recalls another competition where a far more experienced team rapidly defeated her new players. She recounts with pride how her female players handled the situation; rather than focusing on the loss, they simply enjoyed the event and supported each other. The culture of Zelda's female-identifying esports community is perhaps reflected in the words of one player: 'In the classroom I have nothing to say, but in esports I feel like everyone is my friend.'

As a gamer herself, Zelda reflects on her own gaming experiences and preference for the narrative, creative and challenging elements of games rather than competitive play. Although Hyrule College's esports program began with a competitive focus, it was through these reflections that Zelda realised the competitive and non-competitive sides of gaming were equally important to build a truly inclusive program. Having previously used *Minecraft* to run design challenges, Zelda was inspired to expand this concept into her school's esports community through *Animal Crossing: New Horizons*, a popular game among her students. The less competitive nature of these challenges was particularly appealing to female students, who were more interested in the creative element. Students' design projects are screencast and displayed around the school, which has resulted in other teachers implementing similar activities in their classrooms.

Zelda highlights the role of library spaces in Hyrule College's esports program, particularly to support female-identifying players. She explains that hosting esports activities in the library, an inclusive space by nature, has helped mitigate players potentially feeling intimidated by technology. Practise sessions are run in library rooms that have no visual access from outside, helping to maintain a sense of privacy and safety. Events are held in a dedicated events space with screens, shoutcasters and other equipment more suitable for audiences. Zelda reflects on how this venue helps reinforce the validity of esports; by using it, 'we're saying, this is important...it becomes really special'.

When asked about managing toxicity in her esports community, Zelda states that sexism is discouraged at school-based competitions. There are strict behaviour policies and processes for managing player conduct. She knows male players can be exposed to sexist comments in other online communities, where 'that's what everyone's doing', without understanding why such attitudes are inappropriate. Much of Zelda's work to address sexism involves calling out inappropriate comments and helping players find different language to express their frustrations. She also comments that her esports community is encouraged to respectfully call each other out, which has strengthened students' emotional regulation skills. Through building a positive culture among players of all genders, Zelda's male players have also learnt how to engage with girls, facilitating respectful friendships between male and female players who share a common interest in gaming.

Maintaining structure and a balance between esports and other activities is an integral part of Zelda's approach to supporting her students. Peer feedback is incorporated into esports coaching, and players must ensure practising esports does not interfere with other academic, social and family commitments. Zelda also encourages her students to remain conscious of their play habits, including the duration of play sessions, the taking of breaks and ensuring their basic needs are being met. She also speaks to the importance of spending time away from screens, encouraging students to go outside and look at trees because 'it's really good for you...and we humans need that'. Ensuring students balance esports with other activities has also helped mitigate families' concerns about unhealthy gaming habits, a frequent barrier to esports participation.

Reflecting on her female players' approach to esports, Zelda contemplates the word 'esports' itself and how its competitive connotation may present a barrier for female players: 'Girls have a different way of looking at...losing and winning, and what the point is of competing.' Creatively focused esports activities, such as design challenges, have been an effective way to address this barrier. Zelda refers to stereotypes about toxic gaming culture, sexism and harassment as other barriers for female-identifying players, but highlights a broader stereotype that 'gaming is for techie people'. This is a significant barrier to inclusive esports among both school staff and students. She explains that having leadership support and assistance from those with experience in school esports has been helpful in breaking down such barriers and building capacity within the school.

## EVERYONE CAN PLAY: RECOMMENDATIONS TO RUN AN ESPORTS PROGRAM THAT SUPPORTS FEMALE PLAYERS

Informed by our own experiences, the advice shared in the case study and the research, the recommendations in Table 3 can serve as a starting point in breaking down gender barriers in your esports program.

## Table 3. Recommendations to Run an Esports Program That Supports Female Players.

| Belonging | Accessibility |
|---|---|
| Formal belonging: | Physical accessibility: |
| • Give female-identifying students the option to play in both mixed-gender and girls-only esports programs and/or competitions<br>• Address gendered stereotypes that may discourage female-identifying players from participating in esports<br>• Girls-only esports programs can be less intimidating for female-identifying players looking to sign up | • Ensure practise spaces are physically accessible and suitably private to ensure others can't see in<br>• Offer game and hardware choices and activity options that cater to a range of physical capabilities and skill levels |
| Informal belonging: | Accessibility to socio-communicative interaction |
| • Foster a safe space "just for us" in girls-only esports programs<br>• Actively combat toxicity and gendered harassment from other players to help female-identifying players feel welcome and protected<br>• Consider and accommodate players' individual circumstances and traits (e.g. ensuring a player who is not used to losing has appropriate support at competitive events) | • Be explicit and clear when explaining activities and expectations in the esports program to help ensure understanding for all players<br>• Provide accommodation and support for different communication preferences within the esports program |
| | Accessibility to interactions in meaningful contexts |
| | • Design esports activities that are meaningful to female-identifying players in the esports program<br>• Ensure players understand why they are participating in an esports activity and what the purpose of the task is<br>• Encourage and be open to feedback from female-identifying players to better understand what contexts are meaningful to them |

| Interaction | Autonomy |
|---|---|
| Opportunity to be a part of a community: | Full autonomy is where students have opportunities to influence form and context: |
| <ul><li>Encourage female-identifying players to communicate with and provide constructive feedback to each other when watching other team members play</li><li>Promote a culture of "girls supporting girls" within girls-only esports programs and/or competitions</li><li>Change the team structures regularly (e.g. each term) to ensure all female-identifying players have the opportunity to participate and be involved</li><li>If you are a gamer yourself, lead by example and wear your identity with pride!</li></ul> | <ul><li>Give female-identifying players the option to choose what type of esports activities they do. Some students might be interested in competitive events, while others might prefer lower-pressure activities such as design challenges</li><li>Encourage student voice and be open to female-identifying players' feedback and suggestions for activities or adjustments that suit their needs</li><li>Empower female-identifying players to openly share what they need to feel safe and comfortable in the esports program</li></ul> |
| **Involvement** | **Acceptance** |
| Subjective experience: | Being acknowledged and accepted by others: |
| <ul><li>Encourage participation for female-identifying students by offering esports activities that accommodate and are meaningful to their individual needs and preferences</li><li>Create a team culture within the esports program that promotes everyone's investment in the team and their success</li><li>Encourage players to balance esports with other activities in meaningful ways (e.g. going on nature walks as a team)</li><li>Consider how female-identifying players might approach winning and losing differently</li></ul> | <ul><li>Encourage female-identifying players to build a supportive culture towards each other within the esports program</li><li>Implement clear boundaries and expectations for how players behave towards each other</li><li>Support confidence and self-acceptance amongst female-identifying players by promoting a mindset of "don't be toxic to yourself"</li><li>Celebrate the successes of female-identifying players amongst the broader school community (e.g. displaying players' design challenge projects around the school)</li></ul> |

# 5

# SUPPORTING NEURODIVERGENT PLAYERS

As our understanding of neurological conditions including autism, attention deficit hyperactivity disorder (ADHD), and dyslexia has expanded, the way we view these diagnostic labels has also changed over time. Strategies to support neurodivergent students have historically followed a medical model focused on addressing perceived areas of skill 'deficit,' particularly in social communication and interaction. By reframing many of the traits associated with these diagnostic labels as differences rather than deficits, the neurodiversity movement has played a key role in reframing how we understand and support these students' needs. Despite this, research shows that neurodivergent students are at increased risk of school distress and/or disengagement, often due to bullying and unmet academic and social needs (Connolly et al., 2023; Granieri et al., 2023).

Gaming is often an area of passion for both neurodivergent and neurotypical children, and video games can support motor, language and social skill development for autistic children (Finke et al., 2015). As such, strength-based programs that harness an interest in gaming can be a way to engage both neurodivergent and neurotypical students around shared experiences. When carefully designed and implemented, these programs can create inclusive, flexible social environments and support neurodivergent students to communicate and build meaningful connections within their school community.

## A BROAD UMBRELLA OF NEURODIVERSITY

As the global inclusive education movement continues to gain momentum, many educators will have heard of the term 'neurodiversity'. While we see this as a positive shift, some glaring misunderstandings of this term remain.

Rather than describing a single difference or condition, neurodivergence is an umbrella term for neurodevelopmental differences, such as ADHD, autism, Tourette's syndrome and dyslexia. These are natural variations in human neurology rather than deficits to be fixed (Kapp et al., 2013). They are neurologies in the minority or 'diverging' from the majority.

More broadly, the neurodiversity movement is inherently political, advocating for society to accept neurological differences as natural, diverse forms of human cognition rather than trying to change the very foundations of a person's identity. Originating in the late 1990s, the movement re-prioritises supports and accommodations that allow neurodivergent individuals to be themselves and thrive in society. In doing so, this movement challenges traditional perceptions of normality, advocating for social and academic inclusion, the universal human right to be true to yourself, and the celebration of cognitive diversity (Pripas-Kapit, 2020; VanDaalen et al., 2024).

The following sections explore some of the labels of difference that are considered neurodivergent. Participants in your esports program may have one or more of these labels, so it's important that you understand modern conceptualisations of these phenomena so you can create a neuroinclusive esports program.

---

**↓↓↑ CHEAT CODE: What is neurodiversity?**

Originally coined by Australian sociologist Judy Singer, the concept of neurodiversity 'refers to the virtually infinite neurocognitive variability within Earth's human population' (Singer, n.d.). In a similar vein to the term biodiversity, neurodiversity reflects 'that every human has a unique nervous system with a unique combination of abilities and needs' (Singer, n.d.).

The neurodiversity framework is a great way to reframe perceived 'deficits' and encourage students to accept and celebrate diversity and difference within an esports program. We are all different in our own ways, and that's a great thing!

---

Autism

Autism is a lifelong neurodevelopmental difference and one of the most well-known diagnostic labels associated with the neurodivergence umbrella. Autism is defined by two key characteristics: differences in social communication and interaction and patterns of repetitive behaviour or restricted interests (American Psychiatric Association [APA], 2013). These defining traits have been established using a medical model, but, importantly, the presentation of autism is highly variable between individual people. Autistic people may have different communication preferences, including speaking, writing, gesture or augmented and alternative communication, and often have a strong preference for structure and a sense of predictability (Reframing Autism, 2023). Many autistic people also show differences in executive functioning and information processing, including their responses to sensory input.

Historical perceptions of autism have focused primarily on a person's 'deficits', but the neurodiversity movement has empowered many autistic people to celebrate their identities and related strengths (Kapp et al., 2013). Autistic people often find great joy in deeply engaging with their interests and might have exceptional knowledge about them (Reframing Autism, 2023). Creative talent, attention to detail, pattern recognition and lateral problem-solving skills may also present areas of strength, along with many others. It's important to remember that every autistic person is unique, with their own strengths and support needs. The best way to support autistic students is to understand them as a holistic individual.

## ADHD

ADHD often co-occurs with other neurodivergences and is characterised by patterns of inattention, hyperactivity and/or impulsivity that impact a person's daily functioning (APA, 2013). Although the presentation of ADHD can be categorised under three main subtypes, individuals can present very differently. Those with predominantly inattentive ADHD often have challenges with maintaining attention and executive functioning tasks such as organisation. Many girls and women with ADHD present with the inattentive subtype but often don't receive a diagnosis or support until later in life, either because they don't fit the stereotype for ADHD or have developed compensatory strategies (Klefsjö et al., 2020). The predominantly hyperactive subtype can present as fidgeting, high energy levels, impulsivity and challenges with self-regulation. Those who have combined presentation ADHD exhibit traits of both inattentive and hyperactive subtypes.

While the differences of ADHD can present challenges for classroom learning, many people with ADHD have unique strengths resulting from their neurotype. One common strength is hyperfocus, where the person concentrates on a single task with such intent that they may not notice the world around them. People with ADHD can also demonstrate strengths in creativity, imagination, observation and problem-solving. In the context of esports, these skills can be particularly helpful for assessing the current gameplay and planning how best to approach in-game tasks.

## Dyslexia

Dyslexia is characterised by challenges with literacy, including spelling, decoding written language and reading with fluency and accuracy. People with dyslexia don't have a cognitive disability; instead, these challenges stem from language skills and the brain's ability to convert between sounds and written symbols (letters) (Australian Dyslexia Association, 2023). Signs of dyslexia often become apparent when learning to read in the early years of school. However, many people with dyslexia use higher level language skills to help them read and compensate for challenges reading single words (Australian Dyslexia Association, 2023). This is especially relevant for girls and women with dyslexia, who often present differently to males and, as a result, are more likely to be formally identified later in life (Arnett et al., 2017). These gender differences also mean that female students with dyslexia are less likely to receive support early in their education.

People with dyslexia are capable of learning and often motivated to read and write, but they might learn best in a different way. Some individuals with dyslexia demonstrate strengths in creative thinking, narrative analysis and taking different approaches to learning (Petrova, 2023). Spatial reasoning, abstract thinking and problem-solving skills are also common areas of strength that have the potential to thrive through participation in inclusive esports programs.

## Other Conditions

While autism, ADHD and dyslexia are well-known examples of neurological differences, anyone whose neurology falls outside the 'typical' is included under the umbrella of neurodivergence (Connolly et al., 2023). Dysgraphia commonly co-occurs with dyslexia and is characterised by challenges with written language skills such as grammar, punctuation and the ability to produce structured, clear and meaningful writing (Chung et al., 2020). Similarly, people with dyscalculia often present with challenges processing numerical information (such as quantities), applying mathematical concepts, including arithmetic, and retrieving mathematical facts (for example, multiplication tables) (Haberstroh & Schulte-Körne, 2019). Although students with these learning differences might experience challenges in some parts of school, access to support that builds on areas of strength such as oral language, creative thinking and memory skills can help these students thrive.

Differences in neurological functioning with physical or motor-based symptoms, including epilepsy, dyspraxia and Tourette's syndrome, are also considered neurodivergences, along with information processing differences such as synaesthesia and sensory processing disorders. The concept of neurodivergence also includes many mental health diagnoses, such as obsessive-compulsive disorder, borderline personality disorder and generalised anxiety disorder. Research has shown high rates of co-occurrence between diagnoses considered neurodivergent, and the traits of individual diagnostic labels may complement or 'mask' each other (Connolly et al., 2023; Rosen et al., 2018). While diagnostic labels can help us better understand neurodivergent students' potential needs, recognising their individual presentations, strengths and challenges is imperative for providing these students with effective support.

## GAMING COMMUNITIES AS SPACES FOR INCLUDING NEURODIVERGENT PLAYERS

Gaming can be stereotyped as a solo recreational activity that offers little opportunity for social interaction. However, this assumption is not necessarily accurate, and gaming communities often provide a setting where players can connect with each other through a common interest. Gaming communities come in many different forms and may be designed to support players of certain demographics (such as women or neurodivergent players) or focus on individual games (such as *Rocket League* or *Valorant*). Many of the most well-known gaming communities focus on popular multiplayer games such as *League of Legends*, but communities also exist around single-player games where fans can discuss the game, share knowledge and provide advice to support other players.

Many large gaming communities operate online, giving players the opportunity to form connections with others who share their interest from all over the world. For neurodivergent players, one of the benefits of online gaming communities is that they offer a range of communication options, allowing players the freedom to communicate in whichever way feels most comfortable for them. These communication options might include text chat, voice chat, in-game gestures, emotes or leaving notes in the in-game world. This is particularly valuable for autistic players who might communicate in different ways or prefer a specific communication method. By design, online gaming communities can support neurodivergent players to engage on their terms by giving them the power to choose when and how they communicate.

Cooperative and team-based games generally have defined game mechanics and clear boundaries that explicitly indicate what players can and cannot do in the game. These characteristics often align well with the needs of neuro-divergent players who thrive in structured settings with clear expectations. Many neurodivergent children also deeply engage with their interests, and a passion for gaming often presents an area of strength. Neurodivergent gamers may develop comprehensive knowledge of their favourite games, including detailed understanding of game mechanics, secrets and 'exploits' to make the game function in unexpected ways. This knowledge is often supported by vocabulary and language specific to gaming that is mutually understood by others who share an interest in video games. In the context of multiplayer gaming and esports, such expertise can be a great asset to the collective team, providing opportunities for neurodivergent players to share their knowledge and teach other players. By creating the conditions for neurodivergent players to adopt strength-based leadership roles, gaming spaces can promote a sense of belonging to an inclusive community where their individual differences are celebrated and valued.

In the school community, esports can be a powerful tool to support social inclusion for neurodivergent students through harnessing an area of interest in video games. Strength-based esports programs can create the ideal conditions for neurodivergent students to engage in collaborative group tasks and develop social connections with peers who share a mutual interest in gaming. The flexible nature of in-game communication options is not only valuable to support neurodivergent players' autonomy but also encourages other players to accommodate and work with different communication preferences. By creating inclusive esports programs that promote a sense of safety and belonging, we can support neurodivergent students to develop relationships, skills and a positive self-identity that extends beyond the esports program to other aspects of their schooling.

## Challenges Experienced by Neurodivergent Players in Gaming Communities

Gaming spaces can promote social connection and a sense of belonging, however, neurodivergent players can also experience challenges when engaging with these communities. Online community users are likely to witness or be subjected to harassment and bullying, particularly through verbal or written means. In some gaming communities, labels associated with neurodivergence (such as 'autistic') are used as an insult or have been incorporated as part of regular 'trash talk' between players. Community members might also use other ableist language, including slurs historically used to describe people with intellectual disabilities, to harass other players. By using neurodivergent identities as derogatory terms, online gaming spaces may send a message that neurodivergent players are not welcome in the community and it is not safe for them to play. Players who are neurodivergent might fear being 'found out' and subjected to targeted harassment or exclusion. As discussed in Chapter 1, the *Autcraft* server was developed to address ongoing harassment towards autistic players in publicly accessible *Minecraft* servers. Although ongoing measures are taken to promote safety and inclusion in *Autcraft*, the server has still endured multiple hacking attempts intended to harass its neurodivergent player community.

Neurodivergent players with social communication differences may find it easier to identify overt signs of unacceptable online conduct (such as bullying), but they might find it more challenging to recognise more subtle indicators of inappropriate behaviour. Players who experience social exclusion or loneliness can also be more vulnerable during online interactions with other users who appear to be friendly or a potential source of social connection. Online groomers often follow a pattern of behaviour, initially building trust with the victim by discussing shared interests, providing support (such as homework help) and offering gifts (for example, digital game downloads or in-game items) (Ringenberg et al., 2022). Although these strategies are intended to hide the perpetrator's malicious intent, players who are socially isolated may perceive them as signs of a genuine connection, increasing their susceptibility to experiencing abuse.

It is imperative to remember that inappropriate behaviour can occur in both physical and online spaces. By equipping players with skills and strategies to navigate online communities, we can build their capacity to self-advocate and respond to the challenges that may present in these spaces. Explicitly teaching neurodivergent players the signs a peer might be friendly or unfriendly is equally important in the virtual world as in the physical world. Many games also have features to restrict interactions with other players, block individual users, or report inappropriate behaviour to moderators. While community management functions vary between different games, maintaining an open culture of communication is essential to promoting wellbeing in esports programs. By creating a safe space where players feel comfortable sharing their concerns or discussing potential inappropriate behaviour, we can help neurodivergent players recognise that support is always available if they need it.

---

🎮 **SIDE QUEST: Healthy video gaming: Supporting autistic young people**

Autism advocacy organisation Amaze has developed a range of resources for supporting autistic gamers and promoting safety when gaming, including a glossary of gaming terms and guides to safe gaming. The guides to safe gaming were developed in consultation with two of the authors of this book for people who are not gamers themselves. These guides include strategies to help balance gaming with other responsibilities, identify inappropriate behaviour and maintain online safety.

🔗 https://www.amaze.org.au/support/resources/healthy-video-gaming-supporting-autistic-young-people/

---

## CASE STUDY: NEXT LEVEL COLLABORATION GAMING GROUP

Although not a dedicated esports program per se, Next Level Collaboration provides an exemplar of how neurodivergent players can be supported through strength-based gaming programs. Co-founded in 2020 by two of the authors of this book, this highly structured lunchtime and after-school program is based on doctoral research from the University of Melbourne. The program uses cooperative video games as a tool to teach teamwork skills that are important for everyone to learn, regardless of neurotype, as depicted in Fig. 6. These skills (such as listening to others, taking turns and checking for understanding) can be shown in many different ways while retaining a common functional purpose. This allows participants the flexibility to work towards a common goal in whatever way feels most comfortable for them. An example of this flexibility in action is listening, with some players preferring to indicate they've heard what someone else is saying by giving a thumbs-up

Fig. 6. A Next Level Collaboration Structured Gaming Group in Action.

rather than making direct eye contact as a person speaks to them. As long as both parties understand these differences in social interaction, this is still an effective way of showing someone that you have listened to them.

The Next Level Collaboration program is specifically designed to support neurodivergent students by following a consistent three-stage structure to maintain a sense of predictability and routine. All sessions are facilitated by adults with a lived experience of neurodivergence, including autism and ADHD. During Stage A, participants are explicitly taught key skills for collaborative teamwork, including how these skills can be shown and the contexts in which they can be used. After selecting one collaborative teamwork skill as their goal, participants transition to Stage B gameplay. In this stage, participants move through ongoing cycles of playing a cooperative video game and receiving feedback on their skill use. Program sessions conclude with a guided reflection on participants' collaborative skills (Stage C), both individually and as a team, along with potential areas for improvement in the next session.

The structured nature of the program is supplemented by additional support strategies, particularly visual supports. Many neurodivergent people process visual information more effectively. Visual representations can reduce reliance on language and literacy skills, where neurodivergent players might need additional support. Visual activity schedules not only provide a clear, sequential outline of session activities and expectations but act as a 'grounding' point when transitioning between tasks. Communication cards for players to request help or a break also support participants' autonomy to ask for what they need. This is especially important if participants feel overwhelmed by the use of verbal language; they can simply pass the relevant card to a facilitator instead. Communication cards also offer a more subtle way to seek support for participants who might feel anxious about asking for help in front of their peers. Miniature whiteboards are another resource that give players the freedom to communicate non-verbally through writing, diagrams or drawing their ideas. Participants have also used miniature whiteboards in other ways to support team success, such as creating job rosters for individual team members when planning to approach in-game tasks.

Many Next Level Collaboration participants experience challenges in other areas of their lives, particularly in terms of social inclusion at school. Some participants (often those who have lower levels of academic achievement) are at risk of school disengagement or have high levels of co-occurring anxiety that affect their capacity to participate in other activities. Most Next Level Collaboration participants have tried other social capacity-building programs or other group-based activities but often had negative experiences as these programs were not neurodiversity-affirming or did not align with their interests. Placing neurodivergent adults at the forefront of session delivery has mitigated many of these challenges. These role models not only share the participants' interest in gaming but also understand and can relate to their experiences. Additionally, neurodivergent session facilitators demonstrate that diversity is something to be celebrated and success in adulthood is possible, helping to combat the negative messaging some participants have previously received. Session facilitators are positioned to lead by example in understanding and advocating for their needs (such as using sensory tools or different communication strategies) and, in turn, encourage participants to build confidence in their identities and self-advocacy skills to support their own needs.

Although Next Level Collaboration participants are incredibly diverse in their strengths, areas of challenge and individual needs, they share a common passion for gaming. By building on this mutual interest, Next Level Collaboration sessions not only foster skills for collaboration and teamwork but also create a setting where neurodivergent gamers can learn from each other and develop social connections with others like them. 'Expert knowledge' is not only revered by the group but collectively shared within the team setting to promote their success. As participants become more familiar with each other and form relationships, this knowledge sharing often extends to other games and areas of interest outside gaming. The social connections formed between Next Level Collaboration participants have transcended sessions themselves, with many participants meeting up at school or on weekends. Some of these friendships, particularly in the case of female and gender-diverse participants, are still withstanding after both participants ceased attending the program.

It's crucial to note that the skills and relationships gained through the Next Level Collaboration program are not a product of the video games themselves. The games simply provide an engaging and interest-based foundation that, when combined with explicit teaching, appropriate resources and support from facilitators, help create the ideal conditions for inclusion and celebrate individual strengths and differences.

---

**SIDE QUEST: Next Level Collaboration**

Next Level Collaboration is a social enterprise that runs in-person social capacity-building groups for neurodivergent children aged 8–15 in Melbourne, Australia. Teacher training programs are also available for school staff who want to run the program for students in their schools. Next Level Collaboration is a neurodivergent-led organisation, and through its social mission, actively recruits staff with lived experiences of neurodivergence to lead their programs.

*⊘ https://nextlevelcollaboration.com*

---

## EVERYONE CAN PLAY: RECOMMENDATIONS TO RUN A NEURODIVERGENT-INCLUSIVE ESPORTS PROGRAM

Bringing together this case study, the research and our professional experiences, the recommendations in Table 4 will help create a safe and welcoming space for your neurodivergent students.

**Table 4. Recommendations to Run a Neurodivergent-Inclusive Esports Program.**

| Belonging | Accessibility |
|---|---|
| Formal belonging: | Physical accessibility: |
| • Ensure neurodivergent players have equal eligibility for and opportunity to participate in esports activities as their peers<br>• Offer suitable accommodations or adjustments to help neurodivergent players fully participate in esports activities<br>• Promote an esports program setting that celebrates diversity and individuality | • Provide a range of game options that accommodate different skill levels and individual needs (e.g. games that don't have time pressures or require "on the spot" decisions from players)<br>• Provide gaming hardware options that accommodate different levels of fine motor skill<br>• Consider the sensory environment when running esports activities, and offer adjustments and/or easily accessible sensory supports where possible |
| Informal belonging: | Accessibility to socio-communicative interaction |
| • Recognise and celebrate individual players' areas of strength and contributions to the team setting to help neurodivergent players feel that they belong and are valued within the esports program<br>• Foster a collective identity within the esports program where all players are united by a common love of gaming | • Provide accommodations for different communication preferences, including both spoken and non-spoken forms of communication<br>• Miniature whiteboards are a great way to enhance communication for all players<br>• Visual resources such as activity schedules and communication cards can be helpful to support neurodivergent players' understanding |
| | Accessibility to interactions in meaningful contexts |
| | • Maintain clear structure and a sense of predictability to help neurodivergent players know what to expect in esports activities and reduce potential anxiety<br>• Provide explicit instructions for activities and expectations for all players within the esports program<br>• Some neurodivergent players might need a clear, direct explanation of the purpose behind a task and why it is relevant for them |

| Interaction | Autonomy |
|---|---|
| Opportunity to be a part of a community: | Full autonomy is where students have opportunities to influence form and context: |
| <ul><li>Build capacity amongst all students in your esports program to work with different communication preferences and strategies</li><li>Ensure neurodivergent students have access to support throughout collaborative tasks</li><li>Position neurodivergent students in leadership roles by encouraging them to share their 'expert knowledge' on gaming or having them teach others how to play</li></ul> | <ul><li>Support neurodivergent players to choose esports activities that work with their individual areas of strength and need</li><li>Be open to and encourage feedback from neurodivergent players about what they need to thrive in your esports program</li><li>Be aware that some neurodivergent players might feel anxious about asking for help, or need additional support to communicate their needs</li></ul> |
| **Involvement** | **Acceptance** |
| Subjective experience: | Being acknowledged and accepted by others: |
| <ul><li>Incorporating areas of strength and interest can encourage neurodivergent players to maintain motivation and engagement in activities – consider what gaming-adjacent interests your students might have!</li><li>Consider the conditions under which your neurodivergent students thrive, and ensure these are replicated in your esports program (where possible) to promote their involvement</li></ul> | <ul><li>Consistently reinforce that every gamer is welcome and belongs in your esports program</li><li>Foster a culture within your esports program that demonstrates consideration, understanding, and respect towards individual differences</li><li>Ensure any toxic behaviour or bullying is addressed quickly and appropriately</li></ul> |

# 6

# ADAPTING PLAY FOR DIVERSE PHYSICAL NEEDS

Most people who grew up gaming have experienced a poor gaming controller. Whether it was a discount third-party controller with a blister-inducing D-pad or, for the older readers out there, a joystick that failed to bring joy by not recognising every second button input, these experiences can be frustrating. While most players have been able to find a better option, players with physical disabilities have been left out of the conversation about how gaming controllers can make or break the playing experience. Over the past decade, there has been a welcome but long-overdue acknowledgement that gaming interfaces, such as controllers and keyboards, do not meet the needs of these players (Ellis et al., 2022; Ellis & Kao, 2019). Put simply, gamers with diverse physical needs require alternative or adaptive input devices that remove barriers to play, something most gaming companies have failed to recognise.

> ★ RESEARCH POWER-UP: Who gets to play? Disability, open literacy, gaming (Ellis & Kao, 2019)
>
> We highly recommend reading this chapter as a starting point for understanding both the barriers experienced by players with disability in controlling gameplay and how disability is represented (or not) in the games themselves. Ellis and Kao critique research involving players with disability and gaming as often being overly focused on therapeutic outcomes rather than the experiences of the players, with this article being a powerful reminder of the humanity of the young people with whom we work. It's also a timely reminder to engage with our players who have disability in co-identifying solutions to barriers.

Fig. 7. Gamers With Physical Access Needs Are Gamers.

School esports programs are a wonderful vehicle for promoting broader conversations around the reduction of barriers for gamers with physical disabilities and differences in fine and gross motor control. Many spaces for play are still inaccessible for young people who use wheelchairs or who use other aides to assist with walking or movement, which makes feeling part of a group difficult. Think back to your own childhood school playground – how easy was it for someone who used a wheelchair to use the equipment and play alongside their friends? As shown in Fig. 7, we believe that by celebrating diverse ways of playing, schools can actually shift the broader narrative around participation and inclusion, and hopefully expand conceptualisations of how people with physical disabilities can belong to their school community.

## FINDING WAYS FOR PLAYERS WITH ALL PHYSICAL ABILITIES TO PARTICIPATE

Through the *Everyone Can Play* framework, we know that the ability to actually access the space and use a control device to play with peers is essential. When thinking about physical accessibility, people's needs vary, but as with every other label of difference we discuss in this book, we must remember that our players with physical disabilities are individuals. 'One size fits all' solutions seldom work for everyone, all of the time.

## Gross and Fine Motor Needs

Physical disability is a condition resulting in physical limitations lasting at least 1 year. These limitations primarily reflect how societies *respond* to these bodies rather than being solely a matter of personal bodily disorder (Kartal, 2023). Students with physical disabilities might have unique needs when participating in esports programs, given the challenges related to both gross and fine motor skills. Making a distinction between these two types of motor skills is helpful for program facilitators in understanding the types of support a student might require to play.

> **↓↓↑ CHEAT CODE: Gross motor skills**
>
> Gross motor skills pertain to the movement and coordination of larger muscle groups, primarily used for actions like walking, jumping or maintaining posture (Gonzalez et al., 2019).

For esports, accommodations to support gross motor skills might involve seating adjustments, ergonomic considerations for the angle of a footrest or the positioning of gaming equipment to ensure comfortable and prolonged gameplay without causing strain or fatigue. If you're using a game that uses motion controls, such as the *Just Dance* series, these controls can present serious challenges for students with gross motor skills challenges. If you enjoy a motion-controlled boogie, we don't want to kill the music; we'll explore options to circumnavigate these issues with motion controls later in this chapter.

> **↓↓↑ CHEAT CODE: Fine motor skills**
>
> Fine motor skills involve smaller muscle movements that occur in the wrists, hands, fingers, feet and toes. They allow actions such as grasping, drawing or playing video games using a traditional controller (Gonzalez et al., 2019).

According to analysis of the available data by Brons et al. (2021), somewhere between 5% and 10% of primary school-aged children globally demonstrate a delay in the development of fine motor skills. These skills are vital in esports for precise tasks such as button pressing, manoeuvring an analogue stick or using a keyboard and mouse and, in our collective experience, can be more difficult to support than needs relating to gross motor skills. Students with fine motor skills challenges might require adaptive controllers, key remapping, touchscreens or even brain–computer interfaces to participate in esports activities fully (Kartal, 2023). It is not just a question of access to the game but also whether these players feel welcome and safe to use these alternative input devices. Diagnostic labels such as 'clumsy child syndrome', 'minor neurological dysfunction' or 'dyspraxia of childhood' (Mokobane et al., 2019) do little to support the positive self-esteem of the players, and we've found that these individuals are often very anxious to be playing in front of their peers. We want to be clear at this early point in this chapter that using alternative or adaptive controllers or interfaces is not cheating. If this is something raised by a fellow player (or worse, a parent of a fellow player), please be polite but clear that it is about the rights of every young person with a disability.

---

**⬇⬇⬆ CHEAT CODE: Discussing accommodations as universal human rights**

'Thank you for sharing these concerns. We have to remember that most countries have signed up to the United Nations Convention on the Rights of Persons with Disabilities, and one of the rights we need to ensure is that we provide reasonable accommodation for our students with physical disabilities, including alternative controllers so that they can participate in this program (Article 24 of the convention). We just want everyone to be able to play together.'

---

Providing ways of playing that address physical needs not only ensures students with physical disabilities can enjoy esports on a somewhat even playing field, but also highlights the importance of inclusivity and diversity in gaming communities. Adapting to these needs isn't just about fairness; it's about embracing the richness of diverse player experiences.

## Inclusion Is Voice and Choice: Empowering Player Agency When Selecting Hardware

Player voice is pivotal when choosing hardware for your school-based esports program, especially for students with physical accessibility needs. Despite prevailing stereotypes, we know that medicalised labels, such as gross or fine motor skills needs, are only a starting point in understanding the needs and preferences of these players. While one assistive device might be ideal for a particular student, it might be unsuitable or uncomfortable for another. Beyond mere functionality, your young gamers will also have distinct gaming preferences influenced by years of personal experience and comfort with specific hardware. We also need to acknowledge that using a different controller might make some players feel embarrassed in front of their peers. Actively requesting and listening to feedback from the user helps to ensure not only that the hardware meets ergonomic and accessibility requirements, but also aligns with their gaming affinities and social needs.

## Types of Inputs That Can Be Used to Play Games

### Mouse and Keyboard Selection

Supporting players' fine motor skills needs involves giving careful thought to hardware and software that can be used to create an inclusive and enjoyable experience. For example, if you're playing PC games such as *League of Legends*, then the choice of a mouse is paramount. For all players, it's advisable to use ergonomically designed mice that comfortably fit in the player's hand, minimising strain and excessive movement (Dhengre et al., 2023). For some players, the guiding of a physical mouse across a mouse pad can be difficult. In this case, it might be more comfortable to use a trackball mouse. Unlike conventional mice that necessitate moving the entire device to guide the cursor, trackball mice only require the rotation of an internal ball (Standen et al., 2011). While this sounds like a winning solution, using a trackball can make it much slower for the player to dictate precise actions in a fast-moving game like time strategy games. If you ever want to experience extreme frustration, try playing competitive *Starcraft* using a trackball! 'Dots per inch' or 'dots per linear inc' (DPI) are used to measure the sensitivity of a computer mouse's sensor (Smith, 2023). A compromise between accessibility and performance can be opting for a mouse with adjustable DPI settings, enabling users to customise precision levels according to their preference (Boudaoud et al., 2022).

PC gaming often pairs mouse controls with keyboards, so it is also important to think about offering options for keyboards with larger keys or keys demanding minimal force for activation to accommodate players with different fine or gross motor needs. There are specialised keyboards on the market with provisions for customisable layouts, allowing players to arrange keys in configurations that they find most comfortable (Charlie, 2016). Another useful feature is tactile or haptic feedback. Providing a subtle bump or resistance when a key is actuated can aid players in distinguishing successful keypresses.

In terms of software, we find that features like sticky keys, present in many operating systems, can be helpful. This feature permits users to sequentially press keys for shortcuts, removing the need to press multiple keys simultaneously. Key rebinding enables players to assign controls to more accessible keys. Mouse acceleration settings, found in many games, refine how the cursor reacts to mouse movement, potentially making navigation more intuitive. Another crucial software adjustment is the slow keys function. Typically located in accessibility settings, it mandates a prolonged keypress for registration, significantly reducing unintentional activations.

---

**SIDE QUEST: How to make the most of your Windows PC's accessibility features (Baker, 2022)**

This provides a list of accessibility features in Windows 11, where to find each one, and what they can do to make playing (and working) easier for people with a range of needs.

    https://www.theverge.com/23184718/accessibility-windows-pc-microsoft-how-to

---

*Adaptive Controllers*

Adaptive controllers have been getting significant media attention recently, with the much-hyped release of the Xbox version followed belatedly by Sony's own model, co-designed with gamers who have disability (Bunting, 2023). While these devices are both welcome tools for removing barriers for players with disability, it's important to recognise the grassroots innovators who inspired the designs of these controllers (AbleGamers, 2023a). Such input devices have enhanced the accessibility of esports to players with both fine and gross motor skill challenges. Our community owes a debt of gratitude to these pioneers.

---

**SIDE QUEST: AbleGamers (2023b)**

This charity creates opportunities for people with disability to access play in order to combat social isolation. It focuses on creating inclusive communities and improving quality of life for these gamers.

    https://ablegamers.org/impact

---

The shared mission of all adaptive controllers is to break down the barriers of traditional gaming hardware and provide versatile interfaces that cater to a wide array of physical abilities (Kartal, 2023). For players with fine motor skill challenges, tasks such as precisely pushing a button or manoeuvring a joystick can be daunting. Controllers that offer customisable touch-sensitive buttons, variable-resistance joysticks and even sip-and-puff inputs can provide a tailored experience that addresses these challenges. Familiarity plays an important part in allowing users to adapt quickly to a new input device. As a product of co-design with the disability community, the Microsoft adaptative controller features a series of 3.5 mm headphone jacks, allowing compatibility with many switches or large buttons that are commonly used by students with limited use of their arms (Machkovech, 2018). Components like foot pedals and body-sensitive pads can also be easily added to enable players to use larger muscle groups or different parts of their body to control gameplay.

Allowing users to augment the controller with inputs they are already using for other purposes, both in school and more generally, not only saves time in identifying the best setup but also reduces the 'intimidation factor' for players who are not regular gamers (Machkovech, 2018). While these controllers might not be as accurate or efficient as controllers used by their fellow players, in our experience they help to maintain at least a sense of competitive balance and get these students playing.

Furthermore, the modularity of many adaptive controllers allows for near endless configuration possibilities, ensuring that as a player's needs change or as new challenges arise, the controller can evolve alongside them. A player aged 12 years may have very different needs when they are 17 years old. In essence, adaptive controllers are not mere tools; they represent the inclusive spirit of esports. Normalising their use reinforces the notion that the joy of competition and the thrill of the game should be accessible to all, regardless of physical differences.

*Harnessing the Affordances of Touchscreens*

It would be an understatement to say that touchscreen interfaces have revolutionised the inclusivity of esports for players with physical disability. They offer a direct, tactile form of interaction, removing the need for intermediary devices like traditional gaming controllers or mice. In strategy games such as *Civilisation 6*, players using a touchscreen can drag and drop units using simple finger movements rather than needing to move a mouse cursor. There is debate about whether touchscreens are more accessible using fingers or with a stylus. The late Apple co-founder Steve Jobs famously saw the introduction of touchscreens using styluses as a wasted opportunity, arguing that there should be a direct interaction between human and screen. He went as far as making the affordances of direct physical interaction a key focus of his unveiling of the original iPhone (Gershgorn, 2019).

While Jobs was correct in describing the experiences of most players, some individuals benefit greatly from using a stylus to play games on an iPad or when using touch-enabled devices like the Nintendo Wii U gamepad. Research into inclusive gaming interfaces shows that providing students with the option of using a stylus and explicitly modelling how to use it effectively can help for two reasons: it creates a space between the screen and the hand of the player, allowing a greater field of vision; and a thin-tipped stylus allows for more precise input than a finger (Harrison, 2022).

With that caution in mind, there are things that fingers can do that are more challenging when using a stylus. *Street Fighter IV* is actually very playable for most players on a smartphone with a virtual controller interface, but we can't imagine trying to play it with a stylus. Some virtual controllers are only possible because of the introduction of multi-touch capabilities, but again, players with fine motor challenges will likely require physical buttons (Torok et al., 2015). Multi-touch screens that register multiple inputs can use pinch gestures to zoom in on specific game areas or swipe motions to navigate menus swiftly. While most players benefit from these interfaces and they've become normalised on phones, they can be empowering for some players but frustrating for others. For example, a player with limited dexterity can tap directly on game icons instead of navigating with a joystick, but when a player who experiences challenges brings their thumb and index finger together, these pinching motions can be extremely difficult. One solution is to co-play (or co-pilot) a game on a single device with a multi-touch interface, as it allows multiple simultaneous inputs. However, we've found not everyone enjoys this way of playing.

*Motion Controls*

Motion controls, which capture and translate body movements into in-game actions, can be exceptionally empowering for certain players (Johansen et al., 2020). By transforming physical gestures, large or small, into gameplay mechanics, they can allow a more intuitive and immersive gaming experience that can be easier to learn. For players who may have difficulty with traditional button-based controls, such as those with fine motor challenges, this means that a swing of the arm or a tilt of the head can execute in-game actions such as swinging a sword (Johansen et al., 2020). Despite not offering a true 1: 1 recreation of physical actions in the game world, the first time playing *The Legend of Zelda: Twilight Princess* on the Nintendo Wii was a special experience for each of us. This naturalistic interface can level the playing field as players use bodily movements, bypassing the need for intricate button combinations or joystick manipulations.

However, motion controls aren't universally beneficial. For players with certain physical disabilities, especially those impacting gross motor skills or range of motion, these controls can inadvertently create barriers. Asking a player to swing, jump or make gestures using a controller like a Wii Nunchuk might be unfeasible or strenuous, or result in accidental inputs causing frustration (Standen et al., 2011). Motion controls might, therefore, exclude rather than include, making games more challenging or even unplayable for some players. An example of a popular esports series of games that use motion controls is the *Just Dance* series. A focus on precise time and movements can exclude players who struggle with raising their arms or moving their legs in time to the music. We believe that it's a matter of knowing your students and their needs, and ensuring that you offer a range of games with multiple control options (long live the Wii U!).

## Adjustable Furniture

A significant factor in the success of esports programs for players with physical disabilities hinges on the adaptability of the environment to cater to their diverse needs. Herein lies the crucial role of occupational therapists (OTs) in ensuring the furniture and room layout support the unique needs of players with physical disabilities. These allied health professionals possess specialised knowledge in assessing and recommending ergonomic solutions tailored to individual needs (De Jonge et al., 2017). Students with more complex gross motor skill needs might benefit from chairs with enhanced lumbar support or adjustable armrests. Chairs with high backs and neck rests can provide additional support for those who struggle with head and neck control. Height-adjustable desks, which allow for standing or sitting positions, can be beneficial for students who may need to change postures regularly. Additionally, desks with a tilting feature can offer an angled surface, assisting those who may lean or require specific angles for better game control. Tilting monitors are also important because some players with physical disability need to be as close to the monitor as possible, perhaps due to an inability to independently turn their head (Ripetta & Silvestri, 2024).

Beyond the mere functionality of the furniture, it's important that students don't feel isolated or markedly different from their peers. While customisation is essential for accessibility, it's imperative that such modifications don't socially alienate the student. We believe this requires a culture dedicated to celebrating difference and normalising choices across the team. Instead of building a team identity around a singular brand or type of chair or gaming station, it might be more inclusive to promote diversity in choice. This approach not only addresses the needs of students with disabilities but also emphasises the team spirit grounded in individual strengths and choices. Incorporating the player's perspective is invaluable. Seeking feedback from players regarding comfort, functionality and aesthetics helps to ensure that the furniture positions their body in a way that protects their neck and back health, and appeals to the targeted end user (Smith, 2023). In our experiences, when individuals are actively involved in decision-making, they feel a greater sense of ownership and belonging to the esports program.

## CASE STUDY: SANDOVER SPECIAL DEVELOPMENT SCHOOL

For students at Sandover Special Development School (SDS) in Melbourne, Australia, playing traditional team sports like basketball or soccer is challenging due to the diverse range of physical needs in the class. This urban school supports about 70 students aged from six to 18 years, with a wide range of complex needs manifesting from disability. Many students experience challenges with both fine and gross motor skills. Whether because of physical barriers or a lack of interest, these students often don't want to participate in sports. Consequently, they miss out on the immense social benefits and important life lessons that come from playing a sport with or against others.

As the school's Digital Technologies teacher, Samos saw a widespread love of gaming as an opportunity to augment the work already happening in physical education to promote participation in team sports. Following conversations with the school's OT and physical education teacher, it was decided that cooperative and competitive gaming through an esports program had the potential to get students to play together. Just like the objectives of the school's physical education program, the focus needed to be on finding ways for everyone to be part of the team, regardless of need.

The founding of the Sandover SDS esports program occurred at the height of the *Minecraft* craze in Victorian schools, with the *Minecraft Education Edition* made available to every government school in the region. By positioning *Minecraft* as an esports game, Samos took a game familiar to many students and repositioned it as a team-based competition. Due to the high degree of variability in the students' physical capabilities, direct player versus player battles needed to be minimised in the program. Rather than playing in survival mode, the school launched a series of 'build battles'. For those unfamiliar with this form of competition, build battles involve players working in teams to build something in

Adapting Play for Diverse Physical Needs

a limited time. Each build battle will be themed. When the time is up, points are awarded based on a strict set of criteria explained to the players at the beginning of the challenge. Due to the customisation available with the Microsoft adaptive controller, students who want to play but struggle with a traditional mouse and keyboard can use their switches, or large buttons, connected to the adaptive controller. Sometimes, multiple players choose to work together, sharing one adaptive controller with a set of switches.

Prior to the actual competition (run once a month), teams are given opportunities to rehearse their builds and practise using their mode of control. Practise sessions are held twice a week at lunchtime. Teams are purposely kept consistent across the semester to allow players the opportunity to get to know each other, develop a shared understanding of strategies for planning and creating their builds and hopefully support the development of sustainable friendships that extend beyond the esports program.

Critical to the success of the program has been finding a controller that allowed customisation and provided opportunities for practise using these input devices in low stakes situations, such as informal drop in sessions or well before important tournaments. When the Microsoft adaptive controller became widely available, it was a true game changer, allowing the integration of existing input devices, such as 'Big Mac' buttons, with which both the students and teaching support staff were familiar. By avoiding direct player versus player combat, it was easier to adjust teams to include players with a range of abilities and building speeds, ensuring that no one player stood out as disadvantaged in the eyes of their peers. Being able to export and 3D print the creations from the build battles also allowed every player to be celebrated beyond the outcome of the competition, encouraging less confident players to engage with the program and become part of the school's esports community.

## EVERYONE CAN PLAY: RECOMMENDATIONS FOR INCLUDING PLAYERS WITH DIVERSE PHYSICAL NEEDS

Building on this review of the literature, the experiences shared through the case study and our own time spent supporting players with physical access needs, we've compiled the following recommendations in Table 5 to support students with fine and gross motor skill differences in your program.

**Table 5. Recommendations for Including Players With Diverse Physical Needs.**

| Belonging | Accessibility |
| --- | --- |
| Formal belonging: | Physical accessibility: |
| • Work with allied health professionals, such as occupational therapists, to ensure that all players have access to range of controller options that meet a range of fine gross motor skill needs | • Find out which alternative modes of input are being used by students in your school, and use social media or the community of accessible gaming groups (such as AbleGamers) to find out which interfaces are compatible |
| Informal belonging: | Accessibility to socio-communicative interaction |
| • Model playing using a range of controllers, making clear that there is no one set input device to play games in your program<br>• Explain to all players how to customise their play space, including furniture, chair, and screen height to model that everyone will have individual preferences and needs | • Test using eye gaze with in-game quick access message or emote communication systems to see whether players using these technologies can communicate effectively with their peers in the heat of play |
|  | Accessibility to interactions in meaningful contexts |
|  | • Facilitate conversations around inclusive play, having your teams develop strategies to accommodate differences in gross and fine motor skills and come up with an inclusion plan as a team (for all players, not just players with physical disability) |

| Interaction | Autonomy |
|---|---|
| Opportunity to be a part of a community: | Full autonomy is where students have opportunities to influence form and context: |
| • Offer a range of game genres that are popular with your players, including some that are turn-based or untimed such as *Hearthstone* or the *Civilisation* series | • Ask players with fine and gross motor skill differences what they need and what they would like to help them feel like they belong in the program, including how the program facilitators and other adults should discuss differences in physical needs |
| Involvement | Acceptance |
| Subjective experience: | Being acknowledged and accepted by others: |
| • Model co-pilot or shared modes of playing, showing that it is a valid way of playing to the group | • Treat players using adaptive controllers and other accessible input devices the same as other players, asking them to also model actions for the group and including them in regular tournament practise sessions |

# 7

# CELEBRATING MULTICULTURALISM THROUGH ESPORTS

Gaming is a truly global interest, with video games being developed and played in almost every country in the world. Cultural understanding and communication have never been more important in uncertain geopolitical times, with the risk of radicalisation being an increasing concern for many communities. For countries that were colonised, there is also increasing recognition of the legitimate rights and grievances of First Nations people who lost both their physical and cultural spaces. The global ubiquity of gaming uniquely positions esports as a means for celebrating multiculturalism and increasing cultural understanding. By using common interests to bring people together, esports allows educators to facilitate discussions addressing misconceptions and misinformation through the positive power of shared gaming experiences.

Games developed by people from different cultural groups provide real opportunities for teachers to facilitate deeper conversations beyond tokenism about our differences and what unites us. By building on positive cultural representations in gaming, as the vehicle to start these conversations, students can be empowered to be proud of their multiple cultural identities. Games that celebrate and accurately represent First Nations cultures can also act as a meaningful starting point for building trust and shared cultural understanding between First Nations students, their families and schools through the inclusion of Elders and other community leaders who have not always felt welcome. While building such a community requires an ongoing commitment to listening and learning to ensure that relationships are maintained far beyond the scope of an esports program, gaming is often helpful in creating a context that brings people together and can start conversations about what reconciliation should look like at the local level.

To help conceptualise the pathway from starting an esports program to building community relationships, it's important that communities learn from each other's successes. The case study of two schools shared in this chapter illustrates how this process has been effective in supporting students from multicultural and First Nations backgrounds. Although this chapter discusses the ways in which gaming can celebrate First Nations culture and identity in an Australian context, these lessons can be transported to other national contexts with displaced and systematically disempowered cultures.

## GAMING AS A TRANSCULTURAL PHENOMENON

As the gaming industry has expanded, video games have become embedded into popular culture across the globe. Technological developments, including online play, have promoted gaming as an accessible way to interact with others around the world. The shared joy obtained through gaming often transcends cultural differences and, in many cases, video games help bridge communication gaps between players from diverse language backgrounds. Many large multiplayer games are designed with communication tools that support player interactions, often with built-in 'menus' of standardised commands or expressions that can be mutually understood by all players. These features generally contain commonly used phrases such as greetings or asking to be revived, and some games provide more expansive options, including emotes or actions performed by a player's avatar. In the case of the mediaeval-inspired multiplayer battle game *Chivalry 2*, players can wave, dance or perform battle cries. Each team is also assigned a unique set of battle cry options, promoting a sense of identity and community among its members. Despite having a global player base, *Chivalry 2's* emote system supports a level of common understanding between its culturally and linguistically diverse players by design.

Some gaming communities have also evolved to develop a 'culture' of their own, understood by players all around the world. In the real-time-based life simulation game *Animal Crossing: New Horizons*, it is common to visit players' islands in the opposing hemisphere in order to access specific seasonal items. However, a general set of expectations exists when visiting another player. Players should walk around the island (as running can damage in-game flowers), ask the host player for permission before purchasing items from the shop and leave via the in-game airport rather than exiting the game. It is also customary to leave Bells (the in-game currency) as a token of appreciation after visiting another player's island to obtain a specific item or sell in-game goods at a higher price. These expectations for 'good island etiquette' remain consistent within the player community and exist outside any cultural norms local to the player's geographic area.

The community surrounding popular esports game *Dota2* has built a vocabulary of game-specific jargon to describe game mechanics, in-game actions and particular strategies. This includes terms such as 'gank' (a strategy where a group of players try to attack enemies by surprise), 'b' (meaning 'back'; used to warn another player they are getting ganked) and 'jungling' (going to the woods to obtain gold and experience systematically). These terms have been adopted by or translated into other languages while retaining a consistent meaning, and the *Dota2* community has developed player guides for translating game-related slang into different languages to understand other players better. *Chivalry 2*, *Animal Crossing: New Horizons* and *Dota2* provide just some examples of how video games can create shared, cross-cultural experiences within their player bases. Games can be powerful tools for including players from different cultural and linguistic backgrounds.

## HOW HAS GAMING CHALLENGED COLONISATION?

The colonisation of Australia over 200 years ago had a considerable impact on the Aboriginal and Torres Strait Islander (also known as Indigenous) people, who were displaced from their homes and mandated to conform with British settlers. This forced assimilation led to a significant loss of language, cultural knowledge and identity among Indigenous communities. Storytelling has played a crucial role in preserving Indigenous cultures (one of the world's oldest) and maintaining the customs and beliefs that colonisation may have otherwise destroyed. It only seems fitting that video games have begun to garner attention as an avenue to continue these storytelling traditions and promote understanding of Indigenous cultures and traditions.

*Innchanted*, a cooperative adventure game by Australian indie developer DragonBear Studios, draws on Indigenous stories, values and lore to build a fantasy world where players run a potion brewery. Written by an Aboriginal Gamilaraay man, the game's narrative is woven with themes of connection to and care for the land and waters of the Earth, a prominent element of many Indigenous beliefs (Smith, 2023). By incorporating Indigenous voices and experiences throughout the development process, *Innchanted* builds on enduring storytelling traditions to help bridge gaps in cultural understanding between Indigenous and non-Indigenous Australians.

Australian game developer Drop Bear Bytes has also incorporated Indigenous knowledge and perspectives into their post-apocalyptic game *Broken Roads* to help combat the historically stereotypical portrayals of Indigenous people in media. Set in Western Australia, *Broken Roads* features authentic environments from the lands of the Noongar people and depicts their culture, language and storytelling traditions. Input from Noongar people, Indigenous Elders and a dedicated Indigenous narrative consultant was actively sought throughout the development process to ensure *Broken Roads* respectfully and accurately represents Noongar and other Indigenous cultures (Smith, 2023). It is through these collaborative design processes that gaming can help challenge colonisation. Not only can games such as *Innchanted* and *Broken Roads* continue storytelling traditions through a new medium, but they also help preserve Indigenous traditions and languages through their incorporation into game design and play.

---

🎮 **SIDE QUEST: The future of games and First Nations storytelling**

This article shares some exciting projects from the games industry that portray Indigenous Australian culture, with a particular focus on storytelling. It includes perspectives from game developers who share the approaches they've taken to ensure accurate representation of Indigenous Australian knowledge. *Innchanted* writer Dane Simpson also reflects on what sharing Indigenous Australian history and culture means to him as a proud Aboriginal Gamilaraay man.

🔗 https://www.kotaku.com.au/2023/07/changing-the-landscape-the-future-of-games-and-first-nations-storytelling

---

## WHAT IS THE ROLE OF COMMUNITY AROUND THE GAMES WE PLAY?

While individual differences between members of a cultural group exist, it is the concept of community that unites them and contributes to the formation of a cultural identity. Community can be defined as 'a group of people with diverse characteristics who are linked by social ties, share common perspectives, and engage in joint action in geographical locations or settings' (MacQueen et al., 2001, p. 1929). Although this definition refers to combined action in particular geographic areas, the advancement of online connectivity has provided people all around the world avenues to connect and collaborate without geographic limitations. By also considering virtual spaces as equally valid 'settings' for unified action, it becomes clear that video games and esports programs create a unique opportunity to build communities through a common passion for gaming.

Despite strong parallels between the defining features of cultural and gaming communities, successfully integrating cultural identity into gaming spaces requires conscious work. Collaborative co-design with community members is arguably seen as the 'gold standard' to create gaming experiences that accurately represent or accommodate cultural beliefs, values and norms. While not a game suitable for esports, Millepede's award-winning mobile game *Motu Ta'e'iloa (Our Special Island)* provides an exemplar of such community partnership. Aimed at young children in Tonga, *Motu Ta'e'iloa* promotes awareness and understanding of nutritious food choices through play-based learning. Ongoing collaboration with the Tongan community was incorporated into the development process to ensure the game appropriately represented Tongan culture and the content resonated with Tongan families. The developers also visited Tonga to run co-design workshops with local representatives and promote community and stakeholder engagement, including visits to 11 pilot schools (Millipede, n.d.). *Motu Ta'e'iloa* garnered a positive reception from teachers and parents in the Tongan community, highlighting the importance of community engagement to successfully incorporate cultural identity into game design and build a surrounding community of support.

---

### 🎮 SIDE QUEST: Motu Ta'e'iloa (Our Special Island)

Millepede's website offers a more in-depth explanation of how they planned, co-designed, developed and evaluated *Motu Ta'e'iloa*. It also includes links to evaluation reports with feedback from Tongan parents and teachers who participated in the pilot program. This expresses appreciation for the game's accurate representation of Tongan culture and celebration of their food, language and traditions.

🔗 https://millipede.com.au/work/our-special-island.html

---

With the ever-growing popularity of video games, communities that marry cultural identity and a common love for gaming have started emerging. Founded by Yorta Yorta and Ngarrindjeri man Cienan Muir, *INDIGINERD* is a platform that promotes Indigenous Australian work in gaming and popular culture. Designed to be an inclusive space, the *INDIGINERD* community welcomes non-Indigenous allies to learn about and celebrate Indigenous creativity. In 2019, *INDIGINERD* hosted Australia's first Indigenous Comic-Con, showcasing Indigenous creativity in gaming, cosplay, music and other facets of popular culture. The example set by communities such as *INDIGINERD* can be adapted into an esports program setting. *INDIGINERD* not only amplifies the voices of Indigenous creators, but has also built a community where a common passion for gaming and popular culture facilitates the sharing of Indigenous cultural knowledge and understanding.

## RADICALISATION THROUGH TOXIC GAMING COMMUNITIES

While the online communities built around gaming can provide networks for knowledge sharing and interest-based connection, there is also a risk of these becoming insulated spaces where toxic behaviour can proliferate. The globally accessible nature of MMO games enables players from diverse cultural backgrounds to play in a shared virtual world, but tensions between players may arise due to real-life cultural differences or historical conflicts. While the Mafia-themed MMO role-playing game *Omerta* is unsuitable for esports, events within its player community highlight the potential relationships between culture in the physical and virtual worlds. Upon the launch of a localised German version of *Omerta*, a large group of Dutch players joined the game with a specific intent to kill off the German player community. This attempted 'cleansing' in the virtual world was motivated by hostility related to the circumstances of the Second World War in the physical world (Jacobs, 2008). In response to this event, Dutch players were banned from the German version of *Omerta* to prevent future incidents and associated player deaths. In the context of esports, *Omerta* provides some key considerations for recognising the complex impact of history when building multicultural communities that promote inclusion and understanding without toxicity.

---

★ **RESEARCH POWER-UP: Multiculturalism and cultural issues in online gaming communities (Jacobs, 2008)**

This article analyses two instances of conflict between players from different cultural communities in *Omerta* (Dutch, German and Turkish). It discusses both conflicts in terms of racism, nationalism and cultural difference and highlights some considerations for managing different cultural values in both physical and virtual multicultural societies.

Many online communities run parallel to gaming interests but are not necessarily exclusive to gaming itself. Reddit, a popular news-sharing site, consists of various smaller 'subreddits' dedicated to specific topics or interests where users can post media and engage in forum-like discussions. One of the most popular subreddits, /r/gaming, discusses gaming and game industry news across all platforms and genres, and a vast range of smaller subreddits exist focusing on individual games and platforms. Although the community-driven nature of Reddit has helped empower gaming fans to connect in dedicated online spaces, it has also given rise to subreddits that promote racism, bigotry and other toxic behaviour. These communities may encourage inappropriate behaviour, including the use of slurs and targeted harassment of specific groups and, in extreme cases, attempts to radicalise new users. When working with students who are passionate gamers, it's crucial to consider the external influences that may be present in gaming-related spaces outside your esports program. Players may incidentally become exposed to these toxic online communities without truly understanding the implications of their ideals. It's vital to ensure students are provided with support and education to understand what constitutes toxic behaviour and why it has no place in a culturally safe esports program.

## PLAY AS A FORCE FOR CULTURAL UNDERSTANDING AND HARMONY

As discussed in the context of Indigenous Australian culture, games can provide an avenue for promoting cultural understanding. Some games may draw on cultural knowledge as part of game design, while others translate folklore or cultural experiences into an accessible medium. One example of this is Clover Studios' acclaimed action-adventure game *Ōkami*, which tells the story of Shinto sun goddess Amaterasu who saved Japan from darkness. *Ōkami* also incorporates other elements of Japanese folklore, including *The Story of the Old Man Who Made Withered Trees to Flower*, referenced by Amaterasu's portrayal as a white wolf with the ability to make trees bloom. With a visual style that bears resemblance to traditional ukiyo-e art, *Ōkami* demonstrates the potential of video games as a means to understand culture and tradition through interactive experience.

While esports players from different cultural backgrounds can demonstrate different play styles and strengths, the collective 'gamer' identity developed through esports often transcends such differences. Lin et al. (2023) found that cultural diversity within esports teams improves the quality of team strategy when such identity becomes prominent. Contexts such as playing on 'home turf' in the physical world or managing challenges within the virtual world (such as last-minute rule changes) were found to promote this sense of team identity. The audience support and familiarity associated with home ground and collaborative strategising required to adapt to rule changes encourage multicultural esports teams to work as a collective group with a common goal, rather than focusing on individual differences. The shared knowledge, vocabulary and social norms within esports communities further encourage this collective identity, making esports a unique platform to bring culturally diverse students together through a universal love of gaming.

> ★ **RESEARCH POWER-UP: Cultural diversity in semi-virtual teams: A multicultural esports team study (Lin et al., 2023)**
>
> This article investigates how esports can promote collective identity among culturally diverse esports teams and the conditions that encourage this collective identity. Although it specifically focuses on *League of Legends*, we believe the considerations presented in this article are relevant for educators seeking to run inclusive esports programs that support students from all cultural backgrounds, regardless of game selection.

## CASE STUDY: PALLET TOWN PRIMARY AND VIRIDIAN CITY SCHOOL

Two schools with multicultural student populations are included in this case study. Pallet Town Primary is a government primary school in Victoria, with 350 students from 43 different language groups. Some students come from very high socio-economic backgrounds, while others are refugees. Pallet Town Primary runs esports as part of a lunchtime program for Grade 5 and 6 students, and the program has gained increasing popularity among students since its inception. School principal Ash and STEM teacher Misty state that the diversity of their school community has been an asset for running a successful esports program with 'quite a massive spread of students who take part'.

Located in Queensland, Viridian City School is also a government primary school, with 66% of the 440 students speaking English as an additional language and 15% identifying as Indigenous Australian. Viridian City School' student population is notably less socio-economically advantaged, with 61% of student families in the bottom quarter of Australia. Viridian City School has been running esports since 2022, participating in The FUSE Cup competitions open to Grade 5 and 6 students. Viridian City School works closely with their local secondary school, which is also involved in esports, and they've recently been invited to participate in *Just Dance* competitions for Grade 4 and 5 students.

Reflecting on the benefits for Pallet Town Primary students, Misty explains that the safe, interest-based environment in the esports program has built confidence and leadership skills, along with student friendships that 'wouldn't usually organically happen'. She adds that esports has supported self-regulation and language skills among students from diverse linguistic backgrounds, as they explicitly learn how to communicate with and support each other through games such as *Mario Kart*, as depicted in Fig. 8. For many Pallet Town Primary students with disability, the structured nature of esports has 'really set [them] up for success' and provided them not only with an opportunity to demonstrate their strengths but also recognise those strengths within themselves. Misty states that diversity is also represented among Pallet Town Primary's student esports leaders, who come from culturally diverse and disability backgrounds, providing 'ways for students to be leaders that wouldn't have had the experience if we hadn't done this program'.

Pallet Town Primary' esports program has not only helped support connections between students, but also across the broader school community.

**Fig. 8. Mario Kart Competitions Have Become a Way for Students From Different Cultural Communities to Come Together Around a Shared Interest.**

Ash explains that many students' families from similar cultural backgrounds have built close relationships, creating a sense of community. Student participation in the esports program has encouraged relationships across these cultural groups, as they connect over a mutual interest in gaming and work towards a common team goal. Ash also says that having adults play video games with the students has strengthened the relationships across the school community. Misty adds that beating Ash at *Mario Kart* has now become the students' 'ultimate goal, and they can do it, unfortunately'.

At Viridian City School, to be eligible to join the esports team, students need to attend school and demonstrate positive behaviour. Esports leader Dawn states that esports participation has motivated many Indigenous Australian students at risk of disengagement to maintain school attendance 'because if you want to be on the team, you have to be here to be able to practise'. The esports program has also helped students develop awareness of their behaviour, encouraging them to 'do the right thing' and reflect on choices that might affect their eligibility for participating in esports at school. Dawn explains that she provides students with regular feedback on their behaviour and explicitly communicates if their eligibility is at risk, as students' behaviour 'needs to be appropriate the whole time, not just the week before' an esports event.

Dawn comments that diversity is ingrained into her school community and her students are 'used to…people in our class different to us', but running an esports program has enabled students to 'see first-hand that anyone from any background can do esports'. Like Pallet Town Primary, Viridian City School' esports program has also facilitated friendships and a supportive culture among its diverse student players. Dawn recalls a *Mario Kart* final where one of her students became overwhelmed with the noise, and a Grade 6 girl 'was kneeling next to him giving him encouragement and supporting him'. She says that her students are passionate about gameplay but 'don't really see that it's also to develop those teamwork skills and online well-being'. Dawn highlights the value of esports for supporting conversations around online safety, particularly for students whose families 'don't speak English, so they don't really have the information to share with their children' at home. Participating in esports has also helped Dawn's students consider future career prospects in the esports industry, and 'it doesn't have to be that their career is the pro gamer, it could be an analyst or a caster'.

When asked about factors that have facilitated the success of Pallet Town Primary' esports program, Misty and Ash reflect on how they've created a culturally safe environment. They describe an 'additive' approach of 'trying to make sure that there's opportunities for all those different groups to be represented within our school grounds'. Ash provides the example of food choices at school events; they offer halal, meat-free and other food options that cater for a range of cultural and religious beliefs. He also highlights the importance of identifying what information and boundaries different cultural groups might need when communicating with families about esports. In one instance, a student's family didn't want their child to be photographed at an esports competition. Ash contacted the event organisers to advocate for the student and their family, ensuring they were still able to participate fully without being in any photos. Language differences often present a challenge when tailoring communication for students' families. Ash states that with such linguistic diversity, 'being able to share information with them in their home language, so that they have the maximum understanding of it is a massive barrier'.

Recalling the early days of her school's esports program, Dawn acknowledges the importance of her administrative team's support and that 'it probably wouldn't have happened if my admin team weren't on board'. This year, Dawn has run the esports program alone, alongside her other teaching commitments, which has been challenging. But, she says, 'it's worth it to see the kids have the opportunity'. Dawn adds that 'having at least a couple of people that can do little parts of it would make it more manageable', especially to provide backup in unexpected situations (for example if she is unwell on the day of an esports event).

Viridian City School has relied on major esports competitions due to a lack of esports interest from locally based primary schools, but Dawn hopes that more primary schools will engage in esports down the track. She looks forward to the evolution of the space, explaining, 'the more that schools are doing it, the more people you have to ask for advice from, or you can do little inter-school competitions'.

Despite working at different schools, Dawn, Ash and Misty all describe the importance of removing financial barriers to enable their culturally diverse students' participation in esports. Ash explains that money is 'quite a stress' for some students' families. Pallet Town Primary 'is prepared to put that money behind this sort of stuff' by covering esports competition fees for participating students. Viridian City School provides similar financial support for students who 'don't come from families with disposable income'. Dawn also drives students to esports competitions in her own car because 'I don't want them to miss out' if they can't access transport. The staff from both schools also recognise that not all students have access to gaming equipment at home, so they've ensured esports participation doesn't rely on practising at home. Both Pallet Town Primary and Viridian City School run esports practise sessions at lunchtime, and Misty has organised additional lunchtime sessions for students who 'want to be involved, but may not be at the level of someone that has [a console] at home'. She explains that these sessions are designed to help students learn how to play and practise the game with support from Pallet Town Primary's student esports leaders. Both schools' approaches to supporting their diverse student communities in esports are perhaps best summarised by Dawn: 'It doesn't matter if you're young, old, what language you speak, what culture you're part of. It's just we can all do it.'

## EVERYONE CAN PLAY: RECOMMENDATIONS FOR CELEBRATING MULTICULTURALISM THROUGH ESPORTS

Through implementing the following recommendations in Table 6, program facilitators can celebrate the cultural diversity within their esports communities.

**Table 6. Recommendations for Celebrating Multiculturalism Through Esports.**

| Belonging | Accessibility |
|---|---|
| Formal belonging: | Physical accessibility: |
| • Provide students from all backgrounds with equal opportunity to participate in esports by removing financial barriers where possible<br>• Where possible, provide additional support (such as practise sessions) for students who may not have access to gaming equipment at home<br>• Be explicit about any requirements for students to participate in esports (e.g. maintaining school attendance), and maintain communication about their progress fulfilling these expectations | • Offer game and hardware choices that accommodate a range of physical capabilities and skill levels<br>• Understand that travel requirements may prevent some students from physically attending esports events, and offer travel support where possible (e.g. pre-arranging bus travel for all esports participants or providing a travel allowance to families) |
| Informal belonging: | Accessibility to socio-communicative interaction |
| • Promote diversity and representation of different backgrounds amongst esports student leaders who serve as role models<br>• Encourage players in your esports program to learn from each other about their different cultural backgrounds<br>• Staff participation in esports-adjacent gaming activities (e.g. informal Mario Kart races) can help build relationships between staff and students and promote a sense of belonging within the broader school community | • Consider language differences and provide esports information to families in their home language where possible<br>• Most games released in Australia are localised to English. Consider the extent to which a game relies on English language skills to play and its suitability for players in your esports program |

*(Continued)*

**Table 6.** (*Continued*)

| | Accessibility to interactions in meaningful contexts |
|---|---|
| | • Encourage culturally diverse players to share feedback about the activities and contexts that are meaningful to them<br>• Be explicit when explaining the purpose of esports activities and accommodate any language differences that might affect students' understanding<br>• When communicating with families, clearly explain the purpose behind and boundaries around esports activities. For example, some families might be uncomfortable with their children playing online, but are happy for them to play local games |
| **Interaction** | **Autonomy** |
| Opportunity to be a part of a community | Full autonomy is where students have opportunities to influence form and context: |
| • Families from similar cultural backgrounds can form local communities with close relationships. Collaborative esports activities can help students understand and build relationships with peers from other cultural communities<br>• Ensure support is available for individual skill, language, and cultural differences when planning and implementing group esports tasks | • Promote student voice amongst culturally diverse players and involve them in decision-making processes within the esports program<br>• Encourage and provide students with a safe space to share any cultural factors that may influence their participation in esports activities (e.g. feeling tired when fasting throughout Ramadan) |

| Involvement | Acceptance |
|---|---|
| Subjective experience: | Being acknowledged and accepted by others: |
| • Esports can be a great way to encourage students' broader school involvement (e.g. maintaining school attendance or completing assignments)<br>• Build a supportive culture within your esports program that encourages participation regardless of skill level or previous experience<br>• Support players to provide each other with encouragement and constructive feedback throughout play | • Recognise and celebrate the cultural diversity within your esports program and foster a team culture that demonstrates consideration and respect towards cultural differences<br>• Have clear boundaries and expectations for players' behaviour, with zero tolerance for racism or other toxic behaviour<br>• Encourage students to be proud of their participation in esports and celebrate their achievements |

# 8

# SUPPORTING REGIONAL, RURAL AND REMOTE PLAYERS

Of all of the labels of marginalisation discussed in this book, the challenges faced by regional, rural and remote communities are among those with which two of the authors have the most lived experience (both Matt and Jess grew up in regional communities). While we don't want to perpetuate false stereotypes and oversimplify the communities we grew up in, we do believe that people living outside of major metropolitan areas are more likely to experience certain challenges. From our time growing up in these communities, we understand that being physically and socially separated from major cities can have an impact on the opportunities available to young people.

For teachers and students trying to introduce something new in any school, whether it be starting an inline hockey team (Matt's teenage rebellion) or an esports program, it can be difficult to build a critical mass of support when there is less diversity and a small pool of potential players. We've seen that this can place a disproportioned burden on a small number of enthusiastic proponents. With schools in regional and rural areas around the world more likely to be financially under-resourced (Kolbe et al., 2021; Preston et al., 2013) and have more difficulty retaining staff (Sullivan et al., 2013), we feel that we must explore these challenges and the ways that passionate esports advocates are addressing them.

Schools in remote regions, such as central Australia or northern Canada, face an even greater challenge in introducing these programs, as the inconsistent telecommunications infrastructure, distance between other schools and the lack of economical transportation can make competition impossible. Geographical isolation occurs in countries with greater landmasses, such as Russia or the United States. It also occurs in geographically smaller countries with mountainous regions, such as Japan or the United Kingdom, with

109

significant time required to travel to major population centres. Therefore, using geographical distance as a measure of isolation presents challenges. To address this, we've partially adopted the Australian Institute of Health and Welfare (2004) definitions, augmented with understandings shared by teachers working in regional, rural and remote communities. While not perfect, we offer these definitions as starting points for discussing the challenges these communities might experience.

---

### ⬇⬇⬆ CHEAT CODE: Our definition of metropolitan areas

State (or provincial) capital cities and metropolitan centres with a population of 100,000 or more (Australian Institute of Health and Welfare, 2004).

---

### ⬇⬇⬆ CHEAT CODE: Our definition of regional areas

City with a population of 50,000–100,000 and at least 1 hour of travel away from a metropolitan area.

---

### ⬇⬇⬆ CHEAT CODE: Our definition of rural areas

Community or town with a population of 20,000–50,000 and at least 2 hours of travel away from a regional area.

---

### ⬇⬇⬆ CHEAT CODE: Our definition of remote areas

Community with a population of less than 5,000 and at least 3 hours of travel away from a rural town.

---

Reading this chapter will not overcome these complex systemic and logistical barriers, but we hope that by sharing the research, our own experiences and the experiences of teachers working in these regions, we can offer pathways forward. This will give students living in regional, rural and remote areas opportunities to access the benefits of high-quality esports programs.

## STRATEGIES TO MINIMISE GEOGRAPHICAL ISOLATION

School can be a lonely place at the best of times, but for students and educators who are physically isolated, it can be particularly lonesome (Downes & Roberts, 2018; Perkins et al., 2021). We see the advent of school-based esports programs as an opportunity to bring together geographically dispersed communities. More than just competitive gaming, these programs can create spaces for students to cultivate a strong sense of belonging and community, both within and outside the physical school. Unlike metropolitan areas where numerous teachers in close proximity are running esports programs, educators working in geographically dispersed schools need to be more creative in developing their professional learning networks. Just as local sporting clubs in many regional communities serve as social hubs, esports communities can create a sense of connection that extends beyond the immediate players to include staff and families, knitting a closer community fabric through shared interests and experiences.

### Bringing Students Together With School Serving as a Community Hub

When you live close to your friends or even just other people your own age, it's easy to take for granted the incidental social interactions that come as a result of this. For students who live on farms or other isolated properties, it can take significantly more planning to spend time with other people with whom you share interests (outside of your family circle). For these students, schools are often the primary way to connect with their peers and to build friendships, but the tyranny of long car or bus rides means that opportunities need to occur during the school day.

From our own experiences in supporting players who are travelling far distances, the timing of when you run your program will be key to determining whether or not it is feasible for these students to participate. After-school esports programs are just not viable for these players unless teachers have permission and are willing to run online training in the evening. Out-of-school training sessions present a whole host of ethical and legal questions around liability (Paget, 2013) and are unlikely to be in accordance with government policy in many jurisdictions. Training sessions in the evening can also compete with homework and have the unintentional side effect of forcing students to stay up late. We are, therefore, advocates of lunchtime programs, with players joining each other in a shared physical space, supervised by staff during their regular working hours.

## Mentoring Within the Community

Students are more resilient in leading when they are placed in contexts where they can draw on and build from their interests (Rashid et al., 2017). They are likely to have pre-existing knowledge about the topic and associated vocabulary and understanding of the cultural norms (Hedges, 2019). For many students, gaming provides this opportunity. In smaller schools, there will most likely be fewer teachers available to run esports programs (Downes & Roberts, 2018), so we encourage you to draw on experienced older students and position them as mentors within your program. In our eyes, this is a win-win scenario for everyone involved. Younger students can be welcomed and supported by their more established seniors, helping to reduce anxieties around the transition to a new school. For older students or students who have been at the school for a longer period of time, this is an opportunity for them to receive training in leadership skills and to allow them to practise those skills in a context that may be more meaningful for them.

Esports can give students opportunities to become leading mentors, even if they haven't been thought of as leaders in other contexts. Having a mentoring relationship that reaches across year levels, regular social groups or even across campuses allows students to connect, which might not occur in other contexts (Willis et al., 2012). For this mentoring relationship to develop, it's important that all leaders understand their role, have clear expectations and receive training from staff on how to be an effective mentor. Mentees also need to understand the role of the mentor and develop the skills to listen and take on feedback constructively (Willis et al., 2012).

We recommend allowing time for junior players to check in with your mentors and talk through some of the situations they may encounter in their sessions before they join your program. This time should be scheduled formally and become part of the routine. Likewise, it's important to allow time at the end of each session for a mentor debrief where they can be encouraged to reflect on what they found were the enablers and the barriers in supporting their mentees. Staff have an important role in coaching the mentors, encouraging patience and highlighting the hidden wins. While a junior player may appear not to improve their performance much during a single session, it's

Supporting Regional, Rural and Remote Players        113

worth reminding mentors that the fact the player persisted in the face of adversity is itself an achievement.

While in-person mentoring is easier for staff to monitor and supervise, it's also not realistic for schools with very small numbers of students or schools that are spread across multiple age-determined campuses. In remote communities, students might, realistically, only have the option of entirely online virtual schools (Barbour & Reeves, 2009). This is where it can be valuable to consider online options for mentoring, as depicted in Fig. 9. But we caution you to work with your school leader, governing authorities and families to

**Fig. 9. An Online Mentoring Program With Geographically Dispersed Players.**

ensure that this is done in a way that protects child safety and aligns with local school policies around online communication.

A dedicated Discord server can provide a safe space for online text and video communication. It's important to get permission from your school leadership to set this server up, as well as a code of conduct for all participants. One of the wonderful benefits of Discord is the use of bots, or artificial intelligence (AI) assistants that can be scripted or set up to monitor chats for keywords and to remind server users of the code of conduct. We've heard of some students setting up unofficial Discord servers for their school-based esports teams, but we would suggest that you strongly discourage this as there are serious questions around oversight responsibilities and liability for your school.

## Stronger Connections With Colleagues and Families Through Streaming

We've heard wonderful stories of esports programs helping to bring together colleagues and families in geographically dispersed regions. One teacher we spoke to in conducting research for this book, described how her program had become a beautiful conduit between home and school, helping people feel connected even when physically many kilometres apart. Virtual meetings and forums where staff and parents can interact, share concerns and receive updates can help provide a voice and allow adults supporting the players to get to know each other. We've heard many instances of families and teachers being invited to join secure virtual watch parties for tournaments, with play streamed through a secure video service such as Cisco's WebEx. Through this medium, families can cheer on teams and feel part of the school community. For regional, rural and remote schools in many jurisdictions, one of the benefits of the COVID-19 lockdown periods was the loosening of restrictions around the use of video-conferencing and streaming software. School staff have also become more adept, out of necessity, in using video-conferencing (Orhan & Beyhan, 2020) and for many educators, this mode of communication has been normalised. A particularly exciting initiative we've seen is rural and remote schools organising online workshops or question-and-answer sessions through which guardians learn about the benefits of esports from the players themselves. For many of these families, the tyranny of distance and the pull of work would have prevented them from coming to a basketball game or a school concert, but live streaming or the recording of these sessions can help them feel included and alleviate guilt about not being present during events that matter to their children.

Supporting Regional, Rural and Remote Players 115

## The Need for Online Professional Learning and Communities of Practice

It's not only students in regional, rural or remote communities who face unique challenges emerging from their geographical isolation. Ongoing professional learning is crucial for all teachers, but for program facilitators who feel isolated, it can be the only space where they can get the affirmation they need to persist in the face of resistance (Carpenter & Munshower, 2020). To address geographically induced social isolation, we advocate that these teachers need access to online professional learning platforms and communities. Esports platforms such as Gameplan (Learn2Esport Global Education, n.d.) provide resources, but they are also a means for educators to connect with other educators with a shared interest in esports through creating a network for professional and social connection. Finding someone else who is facing similar barriers in their school or setting can be incredibly empowering.

We've seen a lot of one-off professional learning sessions but educators who feel alone need persistent structures of support and this leads individual teachers to create personal networks to meet their own goals (Oddone et al., 2019). It can be uncomfortable at first, but we encourage you to take a chance and be vulnerable. Share your feelings and suggest forming a community of practice. These communities can be shaped to become spaces where educators can continuously support each other, sharing their experiences, strategies and interesting research they've found. Using social media to find other educators in a similar position can also be a way of building these connections, but we implore you to remember that platforms like Facebook and X (formerly Twitter) are usually open communities. You need to be cautious in how you describe the challenges you face in your school because it may come back to your school leadership or colleagues. Some jurisdictions have punitive policies about their employees discussing their workplace through social media. With that caution in mind, if you feel like an 'esports island', then you need to be able to reach out to people with whom you can objectively and collaboratively formulate a strategy to win over the powerbrokers in your school.

## Little Things That Can Make a Big Difference

In the inverse of Paul Kelly's famous song 'From little things big things grow', for students in regional, rural and remote communities, it's the issues that might seem like a series of minor inconveniences that can combine to present real barriers in unexpected ways. For example, in supporting students to participate in your school's esports program, it's crucial to work closely with them and their families in planning the competition schedule. In regions where it's difficult or financially unviable to hire additional labour, these students often have responsibilities in supporting their family's livelihood and, in some communities, supporting local food security (Martey et al., 2023). This work can be anything from assisting with fencing repairs on their family's farm to helping drive a tractor during harvest. Responsibilities can often involve caring for younger family members during busier times of the year when their parents are running a small business. Understanding and planning for these unique commitments is essential in creating a flexible and inclusive esports schedule.

Another aspect to consider is the additional costs that rural and remote students and schools incur when travelling to esports competitions in metropolitan areas. While we recognise how exciting a field trip can be, as discussed in Chapter 3, these costs to the individual or the school can be significant. Additional expenses such as accommodation, transportation and entry fees must be considered, as well as competing time constraints placed on the use of available school transportation (Story et al., 2023). For rural schools, we've seen firsthand that the financial burden of providing transportation for long distances can be a major barrier to participation in esports events. When these extra expenses are invoiced to families in a single bill with a short payment period, it can also put a strain on the students' families, making it more difficult for them to support their child's involvement in something that may be seen as a luxury. Schools need to consider these factors and explore possible grant or sponsorship arrangements or deferred payment systems to alleviate these financial challenges.

Telecommunications infrastructure presents another significant challenge for students in regional, rural and remote areas. Often, internet access in these locations is not only more expensive but also comes with higher latency, which can put esports players at a competitive disadvantage (Johnson & Williams, 2023). This disparity in internet quality affects not only the gameplay experience but also the ability of students to train and compete on an equal footing with their peers in urban areas. Addressing these connectivity issues is easier said than done, but it's important to acknowledge that it's not a level playing field. At the end of the day, we believe that all teachers want to ensure that talent and skill are the determining factors in competition, not the quality of a player's internet connection.

Lastly, the geographical isolation of regional, rural and remote communities demands longer term planning. Everything from accessing onsite technical support to shipping new hardware often takes more time. Even downloading updates for games can be a slow process due to slower internet speeds. These challenges require schools to be more organised and proactive than their metropolitan counterparts. Planning needs to be done well in advance, and contingency plans should be in place for technical issues. This demands that staff, at the very least, have enough foundational knowledge of hardware and software to work remotely with technical support over the phone.

## CASE STUDY: ZEBES COLLEGE

Most people wouldn't necessarily think of Zebes College as being geographically disadvantaged. This Catholic secondary school is only about an hour from the nearest major city in Queensland, Australia. It's a new school, opened 7 years ago in a population growth corridor with rapidly increasing numbers of students. So, unlike some regional schools, it's definitely not at risk of dwindling enrolments or being closed anytime soon. In reality, teacher and esports program facilitator Samus contends that Zebes College is still very much a regional school in terms of both infrastructure and the community it serves. The school has a large number of rural students travelling significant distances each day; some travel an hour or more just to get to school. This, notes Samus, can create challenges for consistent attendance. Addressing this issue, she sees her esports program playing a vital role in providing a joyful experience, connecting her community 'face to face' and making school a meaningful place worth attending every day.

Being in a new regional school has presented exciting opportunities for Samus but also some challenges. She's acting in a leadership position and while in the past she's led numerous change management projects, setting up her esports program has been a new experience. Rather than building from something that was already in place, Samus was allowed to start a new program with no legacy. Her esports program uses a student-centred approach that tries to balance a range of needs, which is easier said than done. Samus provides the example of competing sensory needs, with a group of enthusiastic Year 7 students wanting a loud, bombastic experience while others wanted quiet spaces to play and decompress from an otherwise stressful school experience. Students who prefer not to speak can still share the same physical space as their peers but communicate using the in-game text chat functions and emotes.

As the program expanded beyond its initial Year 7 focus to students in older year levels, balancing the needs of the community became more complex. Different groups of students across year levels were interested in different games, with some players being *Mario Kart* aficionados while others were members of a *League of Legends* guild. In reconciling these competing needs and interests, Samus provided options for students in how they preferred to communicate, making it culturally safe to choose the mode that best worked at any point in the session. She has developed a range of 'invite only' programs, targeting particular needs within her community, as well as programs that are open to everyone. Mentoring younger or new players became a key component of her program. Samus describes the organic growth of Year 10 students mentoring younger players, and the esports community becoming a place where new students could develop friendships. Her proudest moments in the program have been seeing students who arrived at the school as socially reserved, becoming more confident, self-advocating and developing friends across year levels.

Of course, being successful at an international tournament also helps in gaining a cultural foothold within your school. Two years ago, Zebes College won an international competition, with many of the players having never won anything prior to that victory. Notably, the international final was streamed to all students throughout the school, helping to cement the validity and cultural capital of the esports program. Such a high profile achievement has meant that school leadership is supporting the growth of the program and moving away from blocking games being played on the school's network. While this is a wonderful outcome, it does highlight the power of external support and recognition in shaping the attitudes and policies governing schools. Unfortunately, not every school esports program will produce a team of international champions.

Despite the successes experienced within the Zebes College esports program, there have been numerous challenges in implementing Samus' vision. Firstly, the provision of services to this expanding region has not kept up with the rapid growth, with inconsistent access to Wi-Fi not experienced in metropolitan schools. Samus had previously worked in wealthier schools, and from early in the design phase of her program she was concerned by the relative lack of resourcing in terms of hardware and staffing. Culturally, this school is also operating in a more conservative social environment, with many families attending the school initially cautious or even concerned about the introduction of gaming into the school. As students get older, Samus notes that many of her players have become more interested in contentious competitive genres like first-person shooters. But it's difficult to justify playing some of the popular professional esports titles in an educational setting. Out of necessity, she has had to assess the possible risks carefully when designing the program, fearing that if she 'stuffed it up', esports in her school would end. It's a difficult balance to offer older students the experiences they are looking for while keeping her school leadership and broader school community supportive of the program.

One of the greatest benefits of the esports programs has been the connections formed between home and school for her regional and rural students, particularly for students at risk of school refusal. While some of Samus' colleagues were not overly enthusiastic about the introduction of esports in the school curriculum, many of these critics have been won over by the positive feedback from the families of participating students. Students look forward to the days they have esports, and the very fact that they willingly coming to school is a relief for parents. Getting some of the more reluctant students through the front gate is the first step in supporting their academic and social growth, which is a shared goal for teachers and families, regardless of how they feel about gaming.

## EVERYONE CAN PLAY: RECOMMENDATIONS FOR SUPPORTING REGIONAL, RURAL AND REMOTE ESPORTS PROGRAMS

Our final set of recommendations, shown in Table 7, will help you support students in geographically dispersed communities.

**Table 7. Recommendations for Supporting Regional, Rural and Remote Esports Programs.**

| Belonging | Accessibility |
|---|---|
| Formal belonging: | Physical accessibility: |
| • Run your esports programs during regular school hours to support participation for students who have long commutes to and from school | • Budget for supporting extended travel and accommodation for tournaments, or identify online or blended tournaments where remote students can participate |
| Informal belonging: | Accessibility to socio-communicative interaction |
| • Introduce a cross-age mentoring system to break down boundaries across year levels in smaller schools, making sure to train the mentors in how to work with their mentees | • Use communication software such as Discord that compresses audio to allow for real-time verbal communication on slower internet connections while also playing a game |
| | Accessibility to interactions in meaningful contexts |
| | • Find other regional, rural, or remote teachers that are running esports programs in similar schools and share advice around how they have made esports a meaningful part of their local community |
| **Interaction** | **Autonomy** |
| Opportunity to be a part of a community: | Full autonomy is where students have opportunities to influence form and context: |
| • Hold virtual meetings and forums where staff and families can interact, share concerns, and receive updates can showcase the great work players are doing within the program and help families to feel a part of the community | • Survey your students about their competing demands to ensure your tournament schedule takes into consideration other responsibilities players might have at different times of the year, with these being particularly important to many rural and remote communities |

| Involvement | Acceptance |
| --- | --- |
| Subjective experience: | Being acknowledged and accepted by others: |
| • Encourage players to stream their sessions to share play with their broader community, and to encourage players to take on complementary roles within your esports program such as broadcasting matches or commentating on the action | • Develop a range of 'invite only' programs targeting particular needs within your community, to ensure that players who may feel isolated in their community can connect with other players with similar life stories or experiences |

# 9

# TAKING THE NEXT STEPS IN ESTABLISHING YOUR INCLUSIVE ESPORTS PROGRAM

If you've made it to this chapter, you're at least curious about esports and community facilitation through the use of video games. You might even be a passionate gamer, with in-depth understanding of the difference between XP and HP (common abbreviations for 'experience points' and 'health points' for the uninitiated). If you work in a school, you also would likely have encountered people who don't share your interest, and are rather cynical of esports becoming a meaningful part of the fabric of your school community.

We understand where these concerns come from, having had these conversations hundreds of times. When we were younger, media reports would often focus on the violence in games, with fears that children would be emulating Mario by jumping on heads and going down pipes. A series of horrific, high-profile mass shootings in US schools have seen games such as *Doom* and *Grand Theft Auto* bear disproportionate levels of blame. As teachers and researchers working with children, these events and the misplaced responses from some leaders break our hearts. In our local Australian media landscape, the end of COVID-19 lockdowns resulted in the media sharing regular tales of students self-imposed social isolation and school refusal (or 'school can't' as we prefer to say), with gaming often seen as the root cause of these behaviours rather than a symptom of a wider mental health epidemic. As the case studies in this book attest, an effective support program requires a unified team approach. It's imperative that you and your school leaders are able to discuss these perceived issues with colleagues and families to address the of video games as learning tools.

We begin this final chapter by acknowledging that, yes, games that are excessively violent, misogynistic or present negative stereotypes of gender and ethnicity do exist. Many games should *not* be played by children and adult-oriented games such as *Grand Theft Auto* have no place in a school. To help you move the discussion beyond stealing cars and evading the police, we share positive examples of games that promote the qualities of teamwork, inclusion and social responsibility. Throughout this chapter, we provide you with the language and research to link these games and esports to the learning benefits offered through the implementation of inclusive programs.

At the end of the day, what connects all educators, school leaders and caregivers is the desire to achieve outstanding academic and social outcomes for all children. Fig. 10 is an illustration of what we see when we visit schools running esports programs, with gaming being a space that brings together all members of the school community.

We believe that the key to these discussions is positioning video games as instructional tools for learning, and explaining the difference between unstructured play and structured, supported play to colleagues and parents. As leaders of esports programs, we need to maintain focus in conversations on the

Fig. 10. Shared Gaming Experiences Can Build Connections Between All School Community Members (Including School Pets).

learning and well-being outcomes when speaking with those who need convincing.

## USING RESEARCH TO ADDRESS CONCERNS ABOUT SCHOOL ESPORTS

As avid gamers, we might not wish to engage with colleagues or parents who hold views on gaming that we see as antiquated or cynical of something that holds a special place in our personal and professional lives. Gaming is part of our identity, so these conversations can be uncomfortable and feel a little personal. However, as professionals, we need to be able to step up and use evidence to counter misdirected arguments. This section discusses the topical areas of violence in video games, the stereotype of the socially isolated gamer and the relationship between esports and screen time.

### Talking About Violence in Some Games

Since the early days of video games, there have been concerns about the impact of depicted and enacted violence on young players. As professionals working with young people, we naturally share these concerns, but as researchers, we also recognise that the games industry has not always been treated fairly. Between the sensational coverage of tragic incidents like the Columbine High School shooting in 1998 and the US Senate inquiry into violent games led by Senators Joe Lieberman and Herb Kohl in 1993 and 1994, discussions of the connection between violent gaming and child development were largely focused on emotional reactions and moral panic rather than evidence (Ferguson & Ivory, 2012). We believe these emotional discussions have continued to have a profound impact on parent perceptions of violent video games, so it's important that you're equipped with both an understanding of the research and the language to address these concerns.

First of all, we highly recommend that you use the games rating system to decide which games you play in your school. Ultimately, professionals working with young people have an obligation to protect their well-being and emotional safety, so we implore you to investigate the content of games closely and check the suggested age brackets for playing these games. Table 8 outlines

**Table 8. A Mapping of Game Rating Systems in Three Regions/Countries.**

| North American rating system (Entertainment Software Rating Board [ESRB], 2024)  🔗 https://www.esrb.org/ratings-guide | Japanese rating system (Computer Entertainment Rating Organization, n.d.)  🔗 https://www.cero.gr.jp/en/publics/index/17 | European and UK rating system (Pan European Game Information, n.d.)  🔗 https://pegi.info/what-do-the-labels-mean |
|---|---|---|
| Everyone: Content is usually suitable for all ages. May contain minimal cartoon, fantasy or mild violence and/or infrequent use of mild language. | CERO A for all ages: Expressions and content subjected to age-specific limitation are not included in the game, thereby being suitable for all ages. | PEGI 3 suitable for all age groups: The game should not contain any sounds or pictures that are likely to frighten young children. A very mild form of violence (in a comical context or a childlike setting) is acceptable. No bad language should be heard. |
| Everyone 10+: Content is generally suitable for ages 10 and up. May contain more cartoon, fantasy or mild violence and/or minimal suggestive themes. | CERO B for 12-year-olds and above: Expression and content suitable only for 12 years and above. | PEGI 7 for ages 7 and up: Game content with scenes or sounds that can be frightening to younger children should fall in this category. Very mild forms of violence (implied, non-detailed, or non-realistic violence) are acceptable for a game with a PEGI 7 rating. |
| Teen: Content is generally suitable for ages 13 and up. May contain violence, suggestive themes, crude humour, minimal blood, simulated gambling and/or infrequent use of strong language. | CERO C for 15-year-olds and above: Expression and content suitable only for 15 years and above. | PEGI 12 for ages 12 and up: Video games that show violence of a slightly more graphic nature towards fantasy characters or non-realistic violence towards human-like characters would fall in this age category. Sexual innuendo or sexual posturing can be present, while any bad language in this category must be mild. |

| | | |
|---|---|---|
| Mature 17+: Content is generally suitable for ages 17 and up. May contain intense violence, blood and gore, sexual content and/or strong language. | CERO D for 17-year-olds and above: Expression and content suitable only for 17-years and above. | PEGI 16 for ages 16 and up: This rating is applied once the depiction of violence (or sexual activity) reaches a stage that looks the same as would be expected in real life. The use of bad language can be more extreme, while the use of tobacco, alcohol or illegal drugs can also be present. |
| Adults Only 18+: Content suitable only for ages 18 and up. May contain prolonged scenes of intense violence, graphic sexual content and/or gambling with real currency. | CERO Z for 18-year-olds and above only: Expression and content suitable only for 18 years and above. (This assumes that the game should not be sold or distributed to those younger than 18 years old). | PEGI 18 for ages 18 and up: The adult classification is applied when the level of violence reaches a stage where it becomes a depiction of gross violence, apparently motiveless killing, or violence towards defenceless characters. The glamorisation of the use of illegal drugs and the simulation of gambling and explicit sexual activity should also fall into this age category. |

the game rating systems in three regions/countries. However, your jurisdiction might use a different system. These are provided as examples of what to look for in digital or physical stores when making purchasing decisions.

If you're still unsure after reviewing the game rating online or on the game box, there are other ways that you can make an informed, professional judgement. The first is to play the game yourself. We highly recommend that esports facilitators do this anyway, as being familiar with a game will help you support new players in your program and better connect with students when talking about their play. We also recognise that many teachers and support staff are under immense time pressure, so a second option is to watch a trailer or 'Let's Play' video on YouTube. Sharing links to game trailers or Let's Play videos with your school leadership and parents is also helpful in promoting an atmosphere of transparency and can help alleviate concerns. As an illustration of why this is important, we once overheard a child describing the very child-friendly cooperative train-building game *Unrailed!* as 'The axe murderer game' because you use an axe (to cut down wood to build train tracks, not your fellow players!).

In addressing concerns about violence, we highly recommend considering only playing games that are deemed 'family-friendly,' even if you work with older children. As shared in Chapter 8's case study, some of the students arriving in your program will be expecting to play first-person shooter games (*Call of Duty* or *Counter-Strike*). In most school systems, allowing the use of these games will quickly result in the end of your program. By clearly articulating the exclusive use of non-violent games to students, families and school leaders, you can set realistic expectations for your players and appease most concerns about violence from external parties.

However, this might not be enough for a small but often loud minority of people. If you do encounter colleagues or staff who wish to have a further conversation about violence in video games, we believe it's important to discuss the research and conditions in which violence in games can be problematic rather than rely on anecdotal evidence. To help you do this, we've included two 'Research power-ups' related to studies into video game violence. As you read these, it's important to remember the focus is on gameplay in general, so we've drawn out the implications for your school-based program from each study.

We hope that these articles help you to reframe discussions in your school to focus on the positive opportunities of age-appropriate gaming in an inclusive and safe environment.

# ★ RESEARCH POWER-UP: Video gaming and children's psychosocial well-being: A longitudinal study (Lobel et al., 2017)

This study asked 194 children (aged 7–11 years) and their parents to self-report on the frequency of play, the ways they played, their preference to play violent video games and their psychosocial health. Self-reports were completed at the beginning and end of a 1-year period. Analysis of these self-reports found that violent gaming was not associated with psychosocial changes or increases in externalising problems, such as challenges with peers. However, findings showed that frequent competitive gaming may be a risk factor for decreasing prosocial behaviour in children who play approximately eight hours or more per week. As a school-based esports facilitator, this study might be helpful in highlighting the importance of teaching students 'responsible gaming' by keeping track of their play time and ensuring that gaming is part of a balanced extracurricular life.

# ★ RESEARCH POWER-UP: Online toxicity as violence in esports: A League of Legends case study (Wearing, 2022)

This case study explores toxicity through the lens of non-physical violence within the online community for the game *League of Legends*, to better understand its causes and potential solutions. Interestingly, this thesis draws on a wider scope of evidence by reviewing research on violence in traditional sports in an attempt to understand community toxicity in esports. It discusses the important steps that can be taken through improvements in esports community moderation and improving community education around sportsmanship. As traditional sports can be more familiar to some adults, we believe that this case study is useful for school-based esports facilitators as it provides a language to help make links between esports and other sports when speaking to concerned school leaders and parents.

## Talking About Social Isolation and Gaming

Beyond the impact of violence and toxic interactions in online spaces, we sometimes hear concerns from school leaders and parents about gaming being a cause of social isolation. In 2022, Matt attended a roundtable on gaming and mobile phone use in schools held by a prominent Australian politician, with a significant amount of time spent debating whether this was actually true. As the discussions between anti-gaming parent activists and researchers progressed, it was suggested that students playing video games during school lunchtime was a cause of social isolation, and the solution was to ban gaming and build more basketball courts. Frankly, playing basketball is a wonderful social opportunity for some students but is inaccessible for many physically disabled students and would be a hotbed of bullying for many young people.

We see lunchtime basketball and lunchtime esports programs as sharing a similar purpose in terms of creating spaces for social connections, so we reject forcing a student to do one over the other. During these periods of unstructured play, agency should be with the young people within the realms of our professional responsibilities. Research shows that for some young people gaming is the only way to connect with others safely (see Ringland, 2019). It's important to remember that (1) esports is a fairly new phenomenon in the minds of many people and (2) the time delay between researchers identifying an interesting phenomenon to study and sharing their findings can be a drawn-out affair. While we're certain that larger scale studies on the impact of school esports programs on social isolation will be published in the near future, but at the time of writing, this remains a space with minimal evidence. Until larger studies are published, we suggest reading and sharing the following research articles to progress these conversations in your school community. This will help stakeholders consider how the affordances of multiplayer gaming, particularly esports, can be harnessed as a tool for social connection.

Through sharing this research and the conversations that emerge, we hope that those who may have fixed views on the isolating nature of gaming will develop a more nuanced understanding of the conditions in which it can bring people together. These research studies might not convince the most ardent cynic, but clearly articulating the reasons for introducing an esports program through the lens of student well-being should at least get you permission to pilot a program to demonstrate the possibilities.

---

★ **RESEARCH POWER-UP: 'Autsome': Fostering an autistic identity in an online Minecraft community for youth with autism (Ringland, 2019)**

In Chapter 1, we introduced the *Autcraft* server, a global *Minecraft* server specifically for autistic players. In Australia, the *YellowCraft* program offers a similar server for neurodivergent girls, women and non-binary players, and a growing number of similar servers are appearing around the world. To counter the narrative around esports, an inherently social activity, we've found it helpful to highlight the case studies shared by Dr Ringland. These explore the lived experiences of *Autcraft* players through a qualitative digital study of an online community. Ringland collected data through in-game chat logs, interviews with children and parents, observing player interactions on the server and in *Autcraft* forum discussions and collating digital artefacts. The analysis highlights the importance of finding a shared community for many neurodivergent young people. We encourage everyone to read this seminal chapter and carefully consider how you can create an *Autcraft*-like experience in your esports program.

**★ RESEARCH POWER-UP:** The risks and rewards of collegiate esports – A multi-case study of gamers in the United States and Italy (Delello, 2023)

A lot of esports research has been conducted in the United States, which is unsurprising given the country's population and number of research institutions. We think it's important to compare esports experiences in different countries. This study does just that by examining a number of case studies from the United States and Italy to explore similarities and differences in how players engage in esports across these two distinct cultural environments. The research team found that very similar proportions of students played esports in the United States (54.7%) and Italy (55.6%), highlighting their transcultural appeal. Although this article explores experiences of esports 'warts and all', the data analysis found that, for participants in both countries, socialisation was an overwhelmingly dominant reason for choosing to play. This finding aligns with the modern cultural significance of gaming for many students described in Chapter 1. It reinforces the opportunity esports presents as a transcultural medium to promote unity and inclusion within schools.

**★ RESEARCH POWER-UP:** Peer–peer relationships: A key factor in enhancing school connectedness and belonging (Gowing, 2019)

While not specifically focused on esports, Gowing's research investigates student perceptions of their sense of belonging and connectedness in relation to their school community, and presents some important findings for you to share. Using focus groups, questionnaires and analysis of diaries, this study sought to understand 336 students' perceptions of what made them feel connected to their school. A key finding was that peer relationships were more important than relationships with teachers and other members of the school community. For certain students reporting low levels of connectedness to their school, peer interactions stood out as the sole positive element of their school life. This aligns with our observations as educators in our day-to-day experiences. Gowing highlights the role of peer relationships in enhancing school attachment and calls for school personnel to facilitate numerous planned and spontaneous opportunities for peer engagement, in and out of the classroom. When explaining the 'why' of introducing esports into your school, we suggest you share this research with your colleagues and position your esports program as one response to this call for greater peer engagement.

## Talking About Excessive Screen Time

With the increasing accessibility of gaming and media technology, screen time has become a topic of debate. Some studies have established links between excessive screen time and negative outcomes. However, there is so much variance in what constitutes 'screen time activities' that it's difficult to generalise such findings to all types of screen time. We believe there is no 'right' amount of screen time, and what matters more than the quantity of screen time is the quality of these activities. Whether screen time constitutes social media, watching movies or playing video games, we should assess the extent to which such activities are providing a positive experience and, if required, implement strategies to help prevent negative experiences. As with any other activity (such as basketball or art), it's also important to ensure a balance exists between screen time and a person's other responsibilities to support overall well-being.

As educators, we can create the conditions for positive screen time in controlled settings, including esports programs. By implementing clear expectations and teaching our students strategies to have a healthy digital diet,

> ★ **RESEARCH POWER-UP:** Active versus passive screen time for young children (Sweetser et al., 2012)
>
> This study uses data obtained through the Australian Government's Longitudinal Study of Australian Children to investigate screen time patterns. Although the children in this study were generally younger than most esports participants, the analysis provided supports the concept that 'not all screen time is equal'. The authors distinguish between active and passive screen time and outline some of the benefits that can be associated with passive screen time activities, including playing video games.

> ★ **RESEARCH POWER-UP:** Not all screen time is created equal: Associations with mental health vary by activity and gender (Twenge & Farley, 2020)
>
> This study compares mental health outcomes for 13–15-year-old children across screen time spent on social media and gaming. It also analyses differences in mental health outcomes between genders, revealing stronger associations between screen time and mental health indicators for girls than boys. Compared to gaming, internet and social media screen time had stronger links with mental health indicators, including depressive symptoms and low self-esteem. This chapter also provides some potential explanations for these differences.

we believe that a healthy balance between gaming and other social activities is perfectly achievable.

## WHICH SYSTEM(S) SHOULD YOU PURCHASE FOR YOUR INCLUSIVE ESPORTS PROGRAM?

If you're new to gaming, it can be daunting to identify which systems you should investigate for your new program or which additional systems you should add to an existing program. To help you answer this question, Table 9 outlines some important considerations. Alongside the description of each system, we've included our personal preferences to help answer the common question we get asked: 'So ... which one should we choose?'

Please remember that these preferences are subjective, so choose the system that seems most appropriate for your local context. A classic example of this is a parent or friend having one of these systems readily available for donation to the school. Given that each system features a dynamic range of titles that you might want to introduce to your program, we suggest that any of these can be a wonderful starting point for a new program. It is also important to understand that companies in the future change their policies and licencing agreements around how their games can be used in school-based esports tournaments.

---

🎮 **SIDE QUEST: Nintendo Tournament Guidelines**

The new Nintendo Tournament Guidelines detail the conditions in which schools all over the world can use Nintendo titles such as *Mario Kart 8 Deluxe*. We suggest you read these closely and think about how they will constrain your esports program, and weigh up these conditions when deciding on which hardware you purchase.

🔗 https://www.nintendo.com.au/legal/community-tournament-guidelines

---

## WHICH GAMES SHOULD YOU BE PLAYING IN YOUR INCLUSIVE ESPORTS PROGRAM?

Every year, thousands of new games are released, many of which feature competitive multiplayer modes. With so much choice, it can be difficult to know where to start. We've collated the following list of 11 games to give you

## Table 9. Introducing the Most Popular Systems for School-Based Esports Programs.

| | Nintendo Switch (released 2017) | Sony PlayStation 5 (released 2020) | Microsoft Xbox Series S/Series X (released 2020) | Windows PC (constant revisions) |
|---|---|---|---|---|
| **Cost(s)** | Mid-tier hardware cost with games spanning from free to expensive. | Expensive hardware cost with games spanning from free to expensive. Available in both digital-only and disc drive versions. | Mid-tier cost for Series S, expensive hardware cost for Series X. Games spanning from free to expensive, however Xbox Game Pass offers a regularly updated library of digital games for a monthly fee. | Cost varies from mid-tier to expensive depending on hardware performance. Games range from free to expensive. |
| **Controller options** | Console includes Joy-Cons, small controllers that offer button inputs, motion controls and haptic (vibration) feedback. These can be difficult for players with fine motor skill challenges or larger hands to use. Other controller options with more traditional inputs are available, including the Switch Pro controller and 8BitDo's Lite SE, which is designed for players with limited physical mobility. | Uses the DualSense, a traditional controller with two analogue sticks, button and trigger inputs and a small track pad. The DualSense has haptic features, which adjust vibration feedback in response to the game. Sony has recently released an accessible controller that can be customised to accommodate the needs of players with physical disabilities. | Both Series S and X include a default controller with dual analogue sticks, buttons, and triggers. A range of other controllers are also supported. The Xbox Adaptive Controller was co-designed with the disability community for players with motor skill challenges and allows for play using switches and buttons. | Windows PCs can be operated with a keyboard and mouse, and are compatible with a range of controllers, including the Xbox wireless controller and third-party Bluetooth gamepads. Adaptive controllers and other assistive technology can also be used with PCs, including switches or eye gaze technology. |
| **Considerations** | Portable design allows the console to be played as a handheld or connected to a screen. | Console is large and can be susceptible to damage from movement or impact. Cross-platform play does not work for some games. The PlayStation 5 is backwards compatible with most PlayStation 4 games. | Series S does not include a disc drive and can only play digital games. Series X is a larger, more powerful console that includes a disc drive. | PCs vary in performance, and lower-end machines may not be capable of running certain games. It's important to check the hardware requirements of individual games to ensure a PC is powerful enough to run them. |
| **Personal preference** | 1st choice due to the portable nature and range of age-appropriate local multiplayer games. | 3rd choice due to risk of damage and having fewer age-appropriate games. | 2nd choice due to hardware accessibility options and flexibility to choose a console model that suits your needs. | 4th choice due to the relatively high entry costs, variations in hardware performance, and need to upgrade over time. |

## Next Steps in Establishing Inclusive Esports Program 135

a starting point by focusing on the practicalities for esports facilitators. This list includes games for a variety of systems, with a range of genres being represented. To help you understand the basics of gameplay, we have also provided a summary of the gameplay goals and accessibility of the game for new players.

## Rocket League

| Gaming system(s) | Game genre | Possible simultaneous players | ESRB rating |
| --- | --- | --- | --- |
| Nintendo Switch, PlayStation 4, Windows, Xbox One, macOS, Linux | 3D vehicular sports | 8 | Everyone |

*Rocket League* is a vehicular soccer video game. Think of it as soccer, but rather than controlling a human player, you drive a rocket-powered car, which is as fun as it sounds. Games can be played with up to eight players assigned to each of the two teams. Players work together to steer their vehicles into position and hit a giant ball into their opponent's goal. With the timer counting down, teams try to score as many goals (and points) as possible. Simple, right? When people talk about *Rocket League*, one of the first things mentioned is often the wild physics engine that allows players to drive up arena walls, jump over opponents, and overshoot the ball due to the momentum behind their vehicles. It's a simple concept that requires a lot of practise to master.

| **Enablers to inclusion:** | **Barriers to inclusion:** |
| --- | --- |
| • Exciting game premise with fun physics is appealing to many players<br>• Relatively simple and familiar game rules based on common knowledge of soccer<br>• Controls to operate the car are quite straightforward | • Although the game rules and controls are relatively simple, gameplay itself can be challenging and manipulating the physics engine requires skill<br>• Fast-paced nature of gameplay can be challenging for students with differences in information processing<br>• Some accessibility features may not work or be permitted at competitive events |

## Pokémon Series

| Gaming system(s) | Game genre | Possible simultaneous players | ESRB rating |
| --- | --- | --- | --- |
| Most Nintendo consoles | Role-playing game/Turn-based battles | Up to 4 per battle | Everyone |

*Pokémon* is a popular series of role-playing video games, with the mainline games developed by Game Freak and published by Nintendo and The Pokémon Company. It debuted in 1996 in Japan with *Pocket Monsters Red* and *Green*, internationally known as *Pokémon Red* and *Blue* versions. Spanning multiple generations on Nintendo's consoles, the latest entries, *Pokémon Scarlet* and *Violet*, were launched in 2022 for the Nintendo Switch. Each generation introduces new Pokémon storylines, characters, items, and gameplay concepts, with remakes of older games typically released a decade later for the current console. The franchise revolves around capturing and training fictional creatures, Pokémon, to battle against other trainers in turn-based combat, continually expanding the universe with each new game release.

| Enablers to inclusion: | Barriers to inclusion: |
| --- | --- |
| • Structured nature of turn-based gameplay is approachable and easy for new players to learn<br>• Large number of Pokémon gives players lots of flexibility to build their teams<br>• Other cooperative gameplay features such as multiplayer picnics can encourage social connections between players | • Multiplayer battles require a separate console and copy of the game for each player<br>• Strategy development requires comprehensive knowledge of different Pokémon types, moves, and the relationships between them<br>• Some players can find turn-based gameplay frustrating or boring |

# Next Steps in Establishing Inclusive Esports Program

## Just Dance Series

| Gaming system(s) | Game genre | Possible simultaneous players | ESRB rating |
|---|---|---|---|
| Nintendo Wii, Wii U, PlayStation 3, 4 and 5, Xbox 360, Xbox One, Xbox Series X/S, iOS, Android, Nintendo Switch, Microsoft Windows, macOS, Stadia | Dancing | Up to 6 on the latest entries (4 on older versions) | Everyone 10+ (due to mature content in some individual songs) |

Who doesn't enjoy watching, if not participating in a good old-fashioned dance-off? *Just Dance* is a multiplayer motion-based dance video game featuring an array of both timeless and contemporary tracks, each accompanied by unique dance routines. As each track plays, participants mimic the moves of on-screen dancers, with move instructions displayed as pictorial icons at the bottom of the screen. Players' precision in executing these moves earns them points, with special 'gold moves' offering bonus points for striking a pose or mastering the most challenging move of the routine. Scoring is based on the accuracy and timing of performing the move, with each participant receiving rankings.

| Enablers to inclusion: | Barriers to inclusion: |
|---|---|
| • Requires no gaming skills and is approachable for inexperienced gamers <br> • Includes adjustable difficulty settings that change the complexity and timing of dance moves <br> • Motion controls are based on gross motor movements, making gameplay more accessible for players with fine motor skill challenges | • Performing dances requires gross motor skills, so this game may not be accessible for students with physical disabilities <br> • Dance-based gameplay may be less appealing to some students <br> • Caution should be taken to ensure song choices are appropriate for the school environment and students' age |

## Mario Kart 8 Deluxe

| Gaming system(s) | Game genre | Possible simultaneous players | ESRB rating |
| --- | --- | --- | --- |
| Nintendo Switch (note: this is an updated release of Mario Kart 8 on the Wii U) | Action/Racing | 4 on a single system, up to 8 through a local wireless connection, 12 online | Everyone |

*Mario Kart 8 Deluxe* is a racing game where participants take on the roles of characters from the Nintendo universe, navigating karts and motorbikes through ingeniously crafted tracks. Players can not only steer their vehicles but also use power-ups collected from item boxes scattered across the track to either disrupt their rivals or boost their own performance. The game offers a choice of four distinct speed settings before commencing a race. With up to 12 racers, either human or AI-controlled, fiercely competing and deploying items, the race dynamics can shift dramatically, with even the most confident racers potentially plummeting from first to last place within seconds. The tracks include unique segments where racers employ hang gliders, engage in underwater racing, or partake in anti-gravity racing, driving on walls and ceilings at certain junctures. Vehicle customisation is an additional feature, allowing players to tailor their racing experience. Despite the chaotic elements and innovative features, *Mario Kart 8 Deluxe* remains an exceptionally well-crafted racing game at its core, with guaranteed enjoyment for students and staff alike.

| Enablers to inclusion: | Barriers to inclusion: |
| --- | --- |
| • Many students are familiar with the *Mario Kart* series and have previous experience with the game<br>• Assist features can be enabled to prevent players driving off the track, which is helpful for new players<br>• Accommodates more simultaneous players than many other local multiplayer games, with the option to choose individual or team-based races | • Unpredictable nature of items can be frustrating for some players (you can go from first to last very quickly if you get hit at the end of a race!)<br>• Some tracks have a lot of visual information (e.g. moving parts or flashing background lights) and it can be challenging for students with differences in information processing to keep up<br>• Anti-gravity sections can trigger motion sickness for some players |

## Minecraft

| Gaming system(s) | Game genre | Possible simultaneous players | ESRB rating |
| --- | --- | --- | --- |
| Java Edition: Windows, Mac, and Linux<br><br>Bedrock Edition: Windows 10 and 11, Xbox One, Xbox Series S and X, PlayStation 4 and 5, Nintendo Switch, Android, iOS, and more | Adventure/Puzzle /First-person sandbox | Almost unlimited, dictated by server limits | Everyone 10+ |

*Minecraft*'s gameplay involves the collection and placement of objects depicted as blocks on a 3D grid. Players can roam the world freely and 'mine' these blocks to relocate them, facilitating the construction of various structures akin to playing with virtual LEGO. *Minecraft* offers several primary game modes: Survival, Creative, Adventure, and Spectator. The Java version of *Minecraft* offers an additional 'Hardcore' mode, which is worth Googling. In esports competitions, Survival and Creative modes are predominantly used. In Survival mode, players are tasked with gathering resources to build structures, craft items and tools, and earn experience points while managing health, hunger, armour, and oxygen levels. Running out of health results in death and a respawn at the starting point. Creative mode is designed for building and experimentation, granting players unlimited access to nearly all blocks and items for immediate use and destruction. Death is virtually impossible as health concerns are non-existent, and players can fly. Build battles using Creative mode are a popular form of esports competition, with individuals or teams timed to construct something and judged based on predetermined criteria.

| Enablers to inclusion: | Barriers to inclusion: |
| --- | --- |
| • Relatively low-cost game with low-performance requirements and allows cross-platform play in Bedrock Edition<br><br>• Simple design using blocks and a grid often works well for players who have challenges with spatial awareness or processing large amounts of visual information<br><br>• Creative activities (such as build battles) can be less daunting for students who don't want the pressure of participating in directly competitive events | • Some players can find the continuous monitoring of player statistics (health, hunger, etc.) in Survival mode stressful or overwhelming<br><br>• Xbox and Nintendo Switch consoles require additional setup to access custom servers, and custom servers do not work on PlayStation consoles<br><br>• Mac computers are only compatible with the Java Edition, which doesn't work with Bedrock Edition servers for cross-platform play |

## Overwatch 2

| Gaming system(s) | Game genre | Possible simultaneous players | ESRB rating |
| --- | --- | --- | --- |
| PlayStation 4 and 5, Nintendo Switch, Microsoft Windows, GeForce Now, Xbox Series X and Series S, Xbox One | Action/First-person shooter | 10 (5 per team) | Teen |

*Overwatch 2* is a hero-based first-person shooter game. Players are divided into two teams, each selecting a 'hero' from a lineup of 35 characters. Yes, we've included a first-person shooter game in this list. We recognise that program facilitators working with older students will be walking a fine line to balance their professional responsibilities with the preferences of their almost-adult players. *Overwatch 2* can offer a compromise, distinguished by its lower level of graphical violence compared to other first-person shooter games. Characters are categorised into classes, each fulfilling a specific role within the team: the 'damage' class focuses on offence, the 'support' class heals and enhances (buffs) allies, and the 'tank' class provides space and protection for teammates. Every character boasts a unique skillset, comprising active, passive, and ultimate abilities. Continuing the legacy of its predecessor, *Overwatch 2* is primarily dedicated to player versus player (PvP) engagements across various modes and maps, offering both casual and competitive ranked play. It introduces a novel PvP mode called 'Push', which is like a virtual tug of war, where teams compete to control a robot moving a payload towards the adversary's side of the map.

| Enablers to inclusion: | Barriers to inclusion: |
| --- | --- |
| <ul><li>Gameplay is often appealing to older players who want a more exciting and challenging game</li><li>Character classes encourage players to establish and coordinate roles within the team to have the best chance of success</li><li>Diversity is well-represented in the heroes, with different body shapes, cultural backgrounds, sexualities, and neurodivergences represented across the character roster</li></ul> | <ul><li>Players must react quickly, coordinating visual information and fine motor skills 'on the spot' to aim and shoot accurately</li><li>It can be a harsh learning curve due to the fast-paced nature of gameplay, particularly if there is a skill gap between players</li><li>The fast-moving, first-person camera can trigger motion sickness for some players</li></ul> |

# Gran Turismo 7

| Gaming system(s) | Game genre | Possible simultaneous players | ESRB rating |
|---|---|---|---|
| PlayStation 4 and 5 | Racing simulator | 4 on one console (with version 1.40 patch), 20 online | Everyone |

Advancing the series' legacy since its 1997 debut on PlayStation 1, *Gran Turismo 7* offers a driving simulation that closely mirrors real motor racing experiences without a red or green shell to be found. It presents a challenging yet rewarding learning curve for newcomers. With meticulous testing and modelling of over 400 cars and more than 90 racetrack layouts, including iconic global tracks, this simulator emphasises precision driving, from navigating competitor-packed fields to mastering track turns and tyre management. Beyond its detailed single-player mode, *Gran Turismo 7* has become integral to esports, utilising its realistic driving physics and vast vehicle selection for competitions that test players' driving skills and strategic planning on a global stage. This blend of immersive gameplay and competitive relevance solidifies its position as the leading racing simulator in both gaming and esports communities (sorry, Forza fans).

| Enablers to inclusion: | Barriers to inclusion: |
|---|---|
| • Players can choose and customise their cars, promoting player autonomy and self-expression<br>• Game rules and controls are very straightforward<br>• Inclusion of real-life locations from around the world can support cultural understanding (e.g. playing on tracks from students' home countries in a multicultural team) | • Gameplay designed to reflect realistic driving can be challenging and requires more practise compared to other racing games<br>• Some students may find gameplay less interesting or exciting than other, less realistic racing games<br>• Game is exclusive to PlayStation consoles, which are costly |

## League of Legends

| Gaming system(s) | Game genre | Possible simultaneous players | ESRB rating |
| --- | --- | --- | --- |
| Microsoft Windows, MacOS | MOBA | 10 (5 per team) | Teen |

*League of Legends* is a MOBA where two teams of five strive to destroy the opponent's Nexus. Players choose from over 140 champions, each with unique abilities, across various roles, such as top laners, mid laners, junglers, ADCs (Attack Damage Carry), and supports. The game unfolds across three main lanes and a jungle, emphasising strategic play, teamwork, and individual skill in champion control and resource management. With a focus on strategic decision-making, objective control, and team fights, gameplay demands a blend of quick thinking and cohesive team strategy. Regular updates and new champion introductions by Riot Games keep the gameplay dynamic, sustaining its popularity in the competitive gaming community.

| Enablers to inclusion: | Barriers to inclusion: |
| --- | --- |
| • Strategic gameplay requires players to take on defined roles and coordinate actions, encouraging team cohesion and identity<br><br>• More complex game mechanics and strategy requirements can appeal to older or more experienced gamers<br><br>• It is one of the most prominent games in esports, with a large community of other players to learn from | • Matches can be unpredictable with tense situations, which can be stressful or overwhelming for some students<br><br>• Matches can end very quickly if there is a major skill gap between the competing teams, which may be upsetting or frustrating for players<br><br>• The difficulty and mechanical complexity of the game makes it generally unsuitable for younger players |

# Next Steps in Establishing Inclusive Esports Program 143

## Super Smash Bros. Ultimate

| Gaming system(s) | Game genre | Possible simultaneous players | ESRB rating |
|---|---|---|---|
| Nintendo Switch | Fighting | 8 on one console, 4 online | Everyone 10+ |

*Super Smash Bros. Ultimate* is a platform fighting game where participants select from a diverse roster of characters, utilising their unique attacks to weaken rivals and eject them from the arena. It's celebrated for its accessibility to newcomers with the mantra "easy to learn, impossible to master", alongside a broad spectrum of game modes for both solo and team play, catering to esports formats. The game distinguishes itself with a line-up of iconic Nintendo characters, each bringing their distinct abilities into combat. This latest edition encompasses every character from previous iterations, making it the most comprehensive version yet. Given its more cartoon-like violence compared to other fighting games, *Super Smash Bros. Ultimate* has found a niche within school-based esports programs. Its less graphic content makes it an ideal choice for educational environments, promoting competitive play that focuses on strategy and skill without the explicitness often associated with the genre.

| Enablers to inclusion: | Barriers to inclusion: |
|---|---|
| • Roster of familiar Nintendo characters can encourage new players to participate or try the game<br>• Unique character abilities encourage players to collaboratively plan and select a team of characters with advantages over their opponents<br>• Match customisation options are available, including changing the duration, item availability, player lives, and other rules to suit individual needs | • Performing moves relies on accurate directional movement of the analogue stick, which requires fine motor skills<br>• Improving skill at the game often takes time and ongoing practise, which can be frustrating for some players<br>• Mechanics such as movement speed and jump height vastly differ between characters, adding an extra layer of challenge |

## Hearthstone

| Gaming system(s) | Game genre | Possible simultaneous players | ESRB rating |
| --- | --- | --- | --- |
| Microsoft Windows, macOS, iOS, Android | Digital card battling game | 2 online | Teen |

*Hearthstone*, a purely digital collectible card game set in the *Warcraft* universe, offers players a turn-based competitive experience that's notably less intense than many other esports titles, including its physical forerunner, *Magic: The Gathering*. Players engage in strategic duels using decks they've customised, deploying a variety of cards to cast spells, summon minions, and more, all governed by a mana system. Each player represents a 'hero' from one of eleven unique *Warcraft* classes, bringing distinct powers and class-specific cards into play. The simplicity and accessibility of *Hearthstone*'s digital format, alongside its free-to-play model, make it appealing to a broad audience, from hardcore gamers to casual players. The game offers a dynamic competitive scene that evolves with the addition of new cards and strategies, making it an ideal entry point for anyone looking to dive into the world of esports without the 'need for speed' requirements of other games.

| Enablers to inclusion: | Barriers to inclusion: |
| --- | --- |
| <ul><li>Turn-based gameplay follows a more relaxed pace with less pressure and intensity</li><li>Various multiplayer game modes are available with different rules and features</li><li>Often appealing to students who are more interested in card or board games than traditional video games</li></ul> | <ul><li>While the basic rules are relatively simple, deeper strategic elements are far more complex to understand and master</li><li>Building decks can take time as new cards must either be crafted or randomly obtained through card packs</li><li>Turns are timed, which can be stressful for some players, particularly those with differences in executive functioning</li></ul> |

## Fortnite

| Gaming system(s) | Game genre | Possible simultaneous players | ESRB rating |
| --- | --- | --- | --- |
| PlayStation 4 and 5, Nintendo Switch, Microsoft Windows, MacOS, Xbox Series X and Series S, Xbox One, Android | Third person action/sandbox | 100 online | Teen |

*Fortnite* is truly a global phenomenon, but we understand why many schools would be hesitant to introduce a game that is best known as a third-person shooter with cartoon violence and zany emote dances. This game has evolved to now include hundreds of games within the *Fortnite* universe, with many of these games not including any shooting at all. The new LEGO world is a hugely popular game that has the potential to rival *Minecraft*. As a dominant cultural space, *Fortnite* often has the major musical artists featuring in their *Fortnite* Festival, with players able to use skins of feature performers such as Eminem and Lady Gaga. As a sign of its popularity, it was included in the Singapore Olympic Esports Series and there are now hundreds of dedicated education-focused experiences being built within the *Fortnite* Universe such as a scavenger hunt through ancient Egypt.

| Enablers to inclusion: | Barriers to inclusion: |
| --- | --- |
| <ul><li>Many students will have prior experience with the game due to its popularity</li><li>Core game is free to play which removes potential economic barriers</li><li>Includes a range of accessibility features such as control remapping and sound visualisation</li></ul> | <ul><li>There may be significant skill gaps between students who have previous experience with the game and those who do not</li><li>Consider how you might manage the optional in-game purchases and conversations around micro-transactions in games</li><li>In-game menus can be confusing and unintuitive to navigate</li></ul> |

Please remember that this list is only a starting point; our recommendations are subjective. If you're looking for more games, we suggest you explore the growing number of websites for school-based esports programs to see what is being played around the world.

> **⌨ SIDE QUEST: High School Esports League (Generation Esports)**
>
> This large US school-based organisation lists the games used in their programs. This can be a helpful resource if you're looking for additional titles.
>
>     🔗 https://www.highschoolesportsleague.com/games

We always encourage student voice and have found conducting a school-wide survey alongside your own research to be a wonderful way to raise the profile of new esports initiatives. When scouting for new titles, both online and through your students, we do suggest you follow the advice in the previous section and ensure any games introduced into your program align with your professional responsibilities and the values of your school. As much fun as *Counter-Strike 2* can be, perhaps opt for another title and save the headshots for your own weekend sessions.

## TAKE A MINUTE TO REMEMBER WHY WE BECAME EDUCATORS

As you finish your preliminary research and begin planning your next steps to establish or augment your inclusive esports program, it's worth stepping back to reflect on the underlying reasons that we choose to be educators working with children and young people. Teaching and working in support roles within a school can be exhausting. When we speak to teachers around the world, we often hear about the impediments they experience in being able to do what they love, which is almost always working with their students. Establishing and sustaining an esports program will not be easy. You will likely come up against bureaucratic hurdles, questions around funding and a need to constantly justify the value of your vision for what your program could become. We urge you to persevere. It's natural to feel frustrated when problems are raised or become apparent; we all have from time to time when trying to get something new off the ground in often political school environments. As you encounter that cynical colleague, that outspoken parent, or a policy limiting the impact of your program, we find it helpful to remember why we chose our line of work. We strive to help all young people feel safe and happy, and to learn so that they can fulfil their potential. But, we know that this is easier for some children than for others. Those from marginalised communities may not even consider school to be a place for them.

We hope that our firm belief in the potential of esports as a global driver for the inclusion of marginalised children is evident throughout this book. For each of the authors of this book, the opportunity to work with children and adults around and through gaming has been genuinely life-changing. As former students who loved gaming but seldom found a space at school, we wish we had these opportunities. Nonetheless, we're glad that future generations will have access to esports programs. Through sharing the research, case studies and the *Everyone Can Play* framework, we hope to broaden participation in esports. More importantly, we want to help you remove barriers to belonging in your community so the next Matt, Jess or Dan coming through your program will have every opportunity to see school as a place they want to be and where they are free to be themselves.

# ABOUT THE AUTHORS

**Dr Matthew Harrison** is an experienced teacher, researcher and digital creator with a passion for utilising technology to enhance social capacity building, belonging and inclusion in education. He has taught in Australia, South Korea and the United Kingdom at primary, secondary and tertiary levels. Matthew is currently a member of the Learning Intervention team and is the co-leader of the Neurodiversity Project at the University of Melbourne. His favourite game is Donkey Kong Country 2 (SNES), and his favourite console is the Sega Saturn.

**Jess Rowlings** is a qualified speech and language pathologist and a researcher at the University of Melbourne who specialises in the design and analysis of video game–based intervention to build social capacity in neurodivergent children. Jess is also the co-founder and CEO of Next Level Collaboration, a social enterprise that runs strength-based programs supporting collaborative skill development and social connection for neurodivergent children using cooperative video games. Jess' work is informed by her lived experiences of autism and ADHD, along with her personal lifelong love of gaming.

**Daniel Aivaliotis-Martinez** is an experienced educational leader with a diverse and vast experience integrating digital technologies and pedagogies in schools across the world. He now focuses on how schools can leverage esports as a mechanism for improving positive gaming habits while also developing the digital well-being of their students. Through The FUSE Cup, Dan highlights the social and community benefits of establishing esports competitions within educational settings and how this plays a role in improving student academic, social and emotional development.

# REFERENCES

Able, H., Sreckovic, M. A., Schultz, T. R., Garwood, J. D., & Sherman, J. (2015). Views from the trenches: Teacher and student supports needed for full inclusion of students with ASD. *Teacher Education and Special Education*, *38*(1), 44–57.

AbleGamers. (2023a). AbleGamers founder Mark Barlet. https://ablegamers. org/mark-barlet

AbleGamers. (2023b). Our mission. https://ablegamers.org/impact

Adu, A. (2023, May 13). Downing Street downtime: How prime ministers like to relax. *The Guardian*. https://www.theguardian.com/politics/2023/may/12/ downing-street-down-time-how-prime-ministers-like-to-relax

Ainscow, M. (2020). Promoting inclusion and equity in education: Lessons from international experiences. *Nordic Journal of Studies in Educational Policy*, *6*(1), 7–16.

Allen, K. A., Cordoba, B. G., Parks, A., & Arslan, G. (2022). Does socioeconomic status moderate the relationship between school belonging and school-related factors in Australia? *Child Indicators Research*, *15*(5), 1741–1759.

Almeida, I. L., Rego, J. F., Teixeira, A. C., & Moreira, M. R. (2022). Social isolation and its impact on child and adolescent development: A systematic review. *Revista Paulista de Pediatria*, *40*, e2020385. https://doi.org/10.1590/ 1984-0462/2022/40/2020385

American Psychiatric Association (APA). (2013). *Diagnostic and statistical manual of mental disorders (DSM-5)*. American Psychiatric Association Publishing.

Anderson, M., & Jiang, J. (2018). *Teens, social media and technology 2018*. Pew Research Center. https://www.pewresearch.org/internet/2018/05/31/ teens-social-media-technology-2018

Arday, J., Zoe Belluigi, D., & Thomas, D. (2021). Attempting to break the chain: Reimaging inclusive pedagogy and decolonising the curriculum within the academy. *Educational Philosophy and Theory, 53*(3), 298–313.

Armitage, R. (2021). Bullying in children: Impact on child health. *BMJ Paediatrics Open, 5*(1), e000939. https://doi.org/10.1136/bmjpo-2020-000939

Arneback, E., & Jämte, J. (2022). How to counteract racism in education – A typology of teachers' anti-racist actions. *Race, Ethnicity and Education, 25*(2), 192–211.

Arnett, A. B., Pennington, B. F., Peterson, R. L., Willcutt, E. G., DeFries, J. C., & Olson, R. K. (2017). Explaining the sex difference in dyslexia. *Journal of Child Psychology and Psychiatry, 58*(6), 719–727. https://doi.org/10.1111/jcpp.12691

Australian Bureau of Statistics [ABS]. (n.d.). *Socio-Economic Indexes for Areas (SEIFA), Australia.* https://www.abs.gov.au/statistics/people/people-and-communities/socio-economic-indexes-areas-seifa-australia/2021#overview

Australian Dyslexia Association. (2023). What is dyslexia? https://dyslexiaassociation.org.au/what-is-dyslexia

Australian Institute of Health and Welfare. (2004). *Rural, regional and remote health: A guide to remoteness classifications* [Report]. Australian Institute of Health and Welfare.

Australian Institute of Health and Welfare. (2021, September 16). *Social isolation and loneliness.* https://www.aihw.gov.au/reports/australias-welfare/social-isolation-and-loneliness-covid-pandemic

Australian Open. (2023, January 23). Australian Open Summer Smash ft. Fortnite is back for 2023. https://ausopen.com/articles/news/australian-open-summer-smash-ft-fortnite-back-2023

Baker, P. (2022, July 12). *How to make the most of your Windows PC's accessibility features.* The Verge. https://www.theverge.com/23184718/accessibility-windows-pc-microsoft-how-to

Barbour, M. K., & Reeves, T. C. (2009). The reality of virtual schools: A review of the literature. *Computers & Education, 52*(2), 402–416.

# References

153

Blake, J. J., Zhou, Q., Kwok, O. M., & Benz, M. R. (2016). Predictors of bullying behavior, victimization, and bully-victim risk among high school students with disabilities. *Remedial and Special Education, 37*(5), 285–295.

Boudaoud, B., Spjut, J., & Kim, J. (2022, August). Mouse sensitivity in first-person targeting tasks. In *2022 IEEE conference on games* (pp. 183–190). IEEE.

Brand, J. E., & Jervis, J. (2021). *Digital Australia 2022.* Interactive Games and Entertainment Association. https://igea.net/wp-content/uploads/2021/10/DA22-Report-FINAL-19-10-21.pdf

British Broadcasting Corporation [BBC]. (2020, July 6). Nintendo condemns alleged abuse in Smash Bros community. https://www.bbc.com/news/technology-53308579

Brons, A., de Schipper, A., Mironcika, S., Toussaint, H., Schouten, B., Bakkes, S., & Kröse, B. (2021). Assessing children's fine motor skills with sensor-augmented toys: Machine learning approach. *Journal of Medical Internet Research, 23*(4), e24237.

Bulatao, R. A., & Anderson, N. B. (2004). *Understanding racial and ethnic differences in health in late life: A research agenda.* National Academies Press.

Bunting, G. (2023, December 11). Sony's new access controller reveals a big problem in adaptive gaming. *Wired.* https://www.wired.com/story/affordable-accessibility-sony-access-microsoft-adaptive-controllers

Butler, S. (2020, July 5). Every sexual assault allegation in the Smash Bros. community (so far). *The Gamer.* https://www.thegamer.com/smash-bros-community-sexual-assault-allegation-nairo-zero

Canning, S., & Betrus, A. (2017). The culture of deep learning in esports: An insider's perspective. *Educational Technology, 57*(2), 65–69.

Carpenter, D., & Munshower, P. (2020). Broadening borders to build better schools: Virtual professional learning communities. *International Journal of Educational Management, 34*(2), 296–314.

Castejon, V., Albisson, G., & Baptiste, S. (2022). Black power and BLM in three commonwealth nations: Australia, New Zealand, Trinidad and Tobago. *Postcolonial Cultures Studies and Essays,* (1), 19–33.

Cemalcilar, Z. (2010). Schools as socialisation contexts: Understanding the impact of school climate factors on students' sense of school belonging. *Applied Psychology, 59*(2), 243–272.

Chapman, T. K., & Hobbel, N. (Eds.). (2022). *Social justice pedagogy across the curriculum: The practice of freedom*. Routledge.

Charlie. (2016, November 19). Keyboards for people with disabilities. *Better Living Through Technology*. https://bltt.org/keyboards-for-disabled-people

Chen, Y.-L., Senande, L. L., Thorsen, M., & Patten, K. (2021). Peer preferences and characteristics of same-group and cross-group social interactions among autistic and non-autistic adolescents. *Autism, 25*(7), 1885–1900. https://doi.org/10.1177/13623613211005918

Cho, A., Tsaasan, A. M., & Steinkuehler, C. (2019, August). The building blocks of an educational esports league: Lessons from year one in orange county high schools. In *Proceedings of the 14th international conference on the foundations of digital games* (pp. 1–11). https://doi.org/10.1145/3337722.3337738

Chung, P. J., Patel, D. R., & Nizami, I. (2020). Disorder of written expression and dysgraphia: Definition, diagnosis, and management. *Translational Pediatrics, 9*(S1). https://doi.org/10.21037/tp.2019.11.01

Common Ground. (2022, October 25). The stolen generations. https://www.commonground.org.au/article/the-stolen-generations

Computer Entertainment Rating Organization. (n.d.). *Rating system*. https://www.cero.gr.jp/en/publics/index/17

Connolly, S. E., Constable, H. L., & Mullally, S. L. (2023). School distress and the school attendance crisis: A story dominated by neurodivergence and unmet need. *Frontiers in Psychiatry, 14*. https://doi.org/10.3389/fpsyt.2023.1237052

Cook, A., Ogden, J., & Winstone, N. (2016). The experiences of learning, friendship and bullying of boys with autism in mainstream and special settings: A qualitative study. *British Journal of Special Education, 43*(3), 250–271.

Cortez, A., McKoy, A., & Lizárraga, J. R. (2022). The future of young Blacktivism: Aesthetics and practices of speculative activism in video game play. *Journal of Futures Studies, 26*(3).

Daniels, T. (2023, December 20). The most viewed esports events of 2023. *Esports Insider*. https://esportsinsider.com/2023/12/most-viewed-esports-events-2023

de Bruin, K., Kestel, E., Francis, M., Forgasz, H., & Fries, R. (2023). *Supporting students significantly behind in literacy and numeracy: A review of evidence-based approaches* [Report]. Australian Education Research

Organisation. https://www.edresearch.edu.au/sites/default/files/2023-05/aero-supporting-students-significantly-behind-literacy-numeracy.pdf

De Jonge, D., Hoyle, M., Layton, N., & Verdonck, M. (2017). The occupational therapist: Enabling activities and participation using assistive technology. In S. Federici & M. Scherer (Eds.), *Assistive technology assessment handbook* (pp. 211–234). CRC Press.

Delello, J. A., McWhorter, R. R., Roberts, P. B., De Giuseppe, T., & Corona, F. (2023). The risks and rewards of collegiate esports: A multi-case study of gamers in the United States and Italy. *International Journal of Gaming and Computer-Mediated Simulations (IJGCMS), 15*(1), 1–22.

Dhengre, N., Rajput, N. S., & Katarne, R. (2023, June). Design of computer mouse based on ergonomic parameters. In *AIP conference proceedings* (Vol. 2760, No. 1). AIP Publishing.

Downes, N., & Roberts, P. (2018). Revisiting the schoolhouse: A literature review on staffing rural, remote and isolated schools in Australia 2004–2016. *Australian and International Journal of Rural Education, 28*(1), 31–54.

Duncan, S. (2016, April 23). The day 'hackers' told 6 year old autistic children that they should 'kill yourself' [Blog]. *Autism from a Father's Point of View.* http://www.stuartduncan.name/autism/the-day-hackers-told-6-year-autistic-children-that-they-should-kill-yourself

Edström, K., Gardelli, V., & Backman, Y. (2022). Inclusion as participation: Mapping the participation model with four different levels of inclusive education. *International Journal of Inclusive Education*, 1–18.

Education and Employment References Committee of the Australian Senate. (2023). *The national trend of school refusal and related matters* [Report]. https://parlinfo.aph.gov.au/parlInfo/download/committees/reportsen/RB000090/toc_pdf/Thenationaltrendofschoolrefusalandrelatedmatters.pdf

Ellis, K., & Kao, K. T. (2019). Who gets to play? Disability, open literacy, gaming. *Cultural Science Journal, 11*(1), 111–125.

Ellis, K., Leaver, T., & Kent, M. (2022). Introduction gaming (and) disability. In K. Ellis, T. Leaver, & M. Kent (Eds.), *Gaming disability* (pp. 1–16). Routledge.

Entertainment Software Rating Board. (2024). Ratings guide. https://www.esrb.org/ratings-guide/

F1 Esports Series. (2022, May 31). F1 Esports Series Women's Wildcard returns for 2022. https://f1esports.com/news/news/2022/05/31/womens-wildcard-2022

Ferfolja, T., & Ullman, J. (2021). Inclusive pedagogies for transgender and gender diverse children: Parents' perspectives on the limits of discourses of bullying and risk in schools. *Pedagogy, Culture & Society*, 29(5), 793–810. https://doi.org/10.1080/14681366.2021.1912158

Ferguson, C. J., & Ivory, J. D. (2012). A futile game: On the prevalence and causes of misguided speculation about the role of violent video games in mass school shootings. In G. W. Muschert & J. Sumiala (Eds.), *School shootings: Mediatized violence in a global age* (pp. 47–67). Emerald Publishing Limited.

Finke, E. H., Hickerson, B., & McLaughlin, E. (2015). Parental intention to support video game play by children with autism spectrum disorder: An application of the theory of planned behavior. *Language, Speech, and Hearing Services in Schools*, 46(2), 154–165. https://doi.org/10.1044/2015_lshss-13-0080

Formosa, J., O'Donnell, N., Horton, E. M., Türkay, S., Mandryk, R. L., Hawks, M., & Johnson, D. (2022). Definitions of esports: A systematic review and thematic analysis. *Proceedings of the ACM on Human-Computer Interaction*, 6, 1–45.

Freitas, B. D. A., Contreras-Espinosa, R. S., & Correia, P. Á. P. (2020). Sponsoring esports to improve brand image. *Scientific Annals of Economics and Business*, 67(4), 495–515.

Gardner, M. (2023, June 1). G2 esports reveals all-women "Rocket League" team for North America. *Forbes*. https://forbes.com/sites/mattgardner1/2023/05/31/g2-esports-reveals-all-women-rocket-league-team-for-north-america/?sh=38a89f8945dd

Gershgorn, D. (2019, March 19). Would Steve Jobs like the iPad today? *Quartz*. https://qz.com/1575481/would-steve-jobs-like-the-ipad-today

Gibson, A. (2021). Urban education esports for equity and access: A case study. In M. Harvey & R. Marlatt (Eds.), *Esports research and its integration in education* (pp. 30–48). IGI Global.

Giulia, M., Olmos, A., Aleotti, F., Ortiz, M., Rubio, M., & Diamantini, D. (2020). Inclusive education in Spain and Italy: Evolution and current debate. *Journal of Inclusive Education in Research and Practice*, 1(1), 1–23.

Goldschmidt-Gjerløw, B., & Trysnes, I. (2020). # MeToo in school: Teachers' and young learners' lived experience of verbal sexual harassment as a pedagogical opportunity. *Human Rights Education Review, 3*(2), 27–48.

Gonzalez, S. L., Alvarez, V., & Nelson, E. L. (2019). Do gross and fine motor skills differentially contribute to language outcomes? A systematic review. *Frontiers in Psychology, 10*, 2670. https://doi.org/10.3389/fpsyg.2019.02670

Göransson, K., & Nilholm, C. (2014). Conceptual diversities and empirical shortcomings – A critical analysis of research on inclusive education. *European Journal of Special Needs Education, 29*(3), 265–280. https://doi.org/10.1080/08856257.2014.933545

Gordon, G. (2008). What is play? In search of a universal definition. *Play and Culture Studies, 8*, 1–21.

Gowing, A. (2019). Peer-peer relationships: A key factor in enhancing school connectedness and belonging. *Educational and Child Psychology, 36*(2), 64–77.

Granieri, J. E., Morton, H. E., Romanczyk, R. G., & Gillis Mattson, J. M. (2023). Profiles of school refusal among neurodivergent youth. *European Education, 55*(3–4), 186–201. https://doi.org/10.1080/10564934.2023.2251013

Greenway, T. (2023). *Diversity and inclusion growing in gaming and esports – Here's why.* Business & Industry. https://www.businessandindustry.co.uk/video-games-esports/diversity-and-inclusion-growing-in-gaming-and-esports-heres-why

Griffith, J. (2023, April 28). Intersectionality revisited – Neurodivergence and the LGBTQ+ community. *The Observer.* https://www.ndsmcobserver.com/article/2023/04/intersectionality-revisited-neurodivergence-and-the-lgbtq-community

Grubb, J. (2017, December 8). Cuphead wins its biggest prize: The praise of Canadian prime minister Justin Trudeau. *Venture Beat.* https://venturebeat.com/pc-gaming/cuphead-wins-its-biggest-prize-the-praise-of-canadian-prime-minister-justin-trudeau

Haberstroh, S., & Schulte-Körne, G. (2019). The diagnosis and treatment of dyscalculia. *Deutsches Ärzteblatt International, 116*(7), 107–114. https://doi.org/10.3238/arztebl.2019.0107

Harrison, M. (2022). *Using video games to level up collaboration for students: A fun, practical way to support social-emotional skills development.* Routledge.

Hedges, H. (2019). The "fullness of life": Learner interests and educational experiences. *Learning, Culture and Social Interaction, 23*, 100258.

Hehir, T., Grindal, T., Freeman, B., Lamoreau, R., Borquaye, Y., & Burke, S. (2016). *A summary of the evidence on inclusive education* [Report]. Instituto Alana.

Heinrich, L. M., & Gullone, E. (2006). The clinical significance of loneliness: A literature review. *Clinical Psychology Review, 26*(6), 695–718. https://doi. org/10.1016/j.cpr.2006.04.002

Hellström, L., Thornberg, R., & Espelage, D. L. (2021). Definitions of bullying. In *The Wiley Blackwell handbook of bullying: A comprehensive and international review of research and intervention* (pp. 2–21). John Wiley & Sons.

Hennen, A. (2021, June 28). The edifice complex has come for esports. *The James G. Martin Center for Academic Renewal.* https://www.jamesgmartin. center/2021/06/the-edifice-complex-has-come-for-esports

Horeck, T., Ringrose, J., Milne, B., & Mendes, K. (2023). # MeToo in British schools: Gendered differences in teenagers' awareness of sexual violence. *European Journal of Cultural Studies.* https://doi.org/10.1177/ 13675494231191490

Jackson, S. J., Pompe, A., & Krieshok, G. (2011, February). Things fall apart: Maintenance, repair, and technology for education initiatives in rural Namibia. In *Proceedings of the 2011 iConference* (pp. 83–90). https://doi.org/ 10.1145/1940761.1940773

Jacobs, M. (2008). Multiculturalism and cultural issues in online gaming communities. *Journal for Cultural Research, 12*(4), 317–334. https://doi.org/ 10.1080/14797580802561182

Janson, U. (2005). *Vad är Delaktighet?: En Diskussion av Olika Innebörder.* Doctoral Thesis, Stockholm University.

Jarvis, J. M., Shute, R. H., Slee, P. T., Murray-Harvey, R., & Dix, K. L. (2011). Promoting mental health through inclusive pedagogy. In *Mental health and wellbeing: Educational perspectives* (pp. 237–248). Shannon Research Press.

Johansen, T. E. B., Strøm, V., Simic, J., & Rike, P. O. (2020). Effectiveness of training with motion-controlled commercial video games for hand and arm function in people with cerebral palsy: A systematic review and meta-analysis. *Journal of Rehabilitation Medicine, 52*(1), 0–10.

Johnson, M. R., & Williams, J. P. (2023). Bottom-up and top-down tensions: Comparing the Australian and Singaporean esports ecosystems. In F. Gilardi & P. Martin (Eds.), *Esports in the Asia-Pacific: Ecosystem, communities, and identities* (pp. 17–38). Springer Nature.

Kapp, S. K., Gillespie-Lynch, K., Sherman, L. E., & Hutman, T. (2013). Deficit, difference, or both? Autism and neurodiversity. *Developmental Psychology, 49*(1), 59–71. https://doi.org/10.1037/a0028353

Kartal, M. (2023). Accessibility technologies in esports and their impact on quality of life in people with physical disabilities. *International Journal of Disabilities Sports and Health Sciences, 6*(1), 464–474.

Katz-Wise, S. L., & Hyde, J. S. (2012). Victimization experiences of lesbian, gay, and bisexual individuals: A meta-analysis. *The Journal of Sex Research, 49*(2–3), 142–167.

Klefsjö, U., Kantzer, A. K., Gillberg, C., & Billstedt, E. (2020). The road to diagnosis and treatment in girls and boys with ADHD—Gender differences in the diagnostic process. *Nordic Journal of Psychiatry, 75*(4), 301–305. https://doi.org/10.1080/08039488.2020.1850859

Kolbe, T., Baker, B. D., Atchison, D., Levin, J., & Harris, P. (2021). The additional cost of operating rural schools: Evidence from Vermont. *AERA Open, 7*. https://doi.org/10.1177/2332858420988868

Kumar, K. (2021). Growth trends in the gaming industry of India. *International Journal of Social Science and Economic Research, 6*(7), 2500–2510.

Lai, M.-C., & Szatmari, P. (2020). Sex and gender impacts on the behavioural presentation and recognition of autism. *Current Opinion in Psychiatry, 33*(2), 117–123. https://doi.org/10.1097/yco.0000000000000575

Learn2Esport Global Education. (n.d.). About Gameplan. https://gameplan.com/about

Liao, S., & Luqiu, L. R. (2022). #MeToo in China: The dynamic of digital activism against sexual assault and harassment in higher education. *Signs: Journal of Women in Culture and Society, 47*(3), 741–764.

Lin, S., Xu, Z., & Xie, Z. (2023). Cultural diversity in semi-virtual teams: A multicultural esports team study. *Journal of International Business Studies, 54*(4), 718–730. https://doi.org/10.1057/s41267-023-00611-4

Lobel, A., Engels, R. C., Stone, L. L., Burk, W. J., & Granic, I. (2017). Video gaming and children's psychosocial wellbeing: A longitudinal study. *Journal of Youth and Adolescence, 46*, 884–897.

Machkovech, S. (2018, May 17). In the lab with Xbox's new Adaptive Controller, which may change gaming forever. *Ars Technica.* https://arstechnica.com/gaming/2018/05/xbox-adaptive-controller-a-bold-answer-to-the-tricky-world-of-accessible-gaming

MacQueen, K. M., McLellan, E., Metzger, D. S., Kegeles, S., Strauss, R. P., Scotti, R., Blanchard, L., & Trotter, R. T. (2001). What is community? An evidence-based definition for participatory public health. *American Journal of Public Health, 91*(12), 1929–1938. https://doi.org/10.2105/ajph.91.12.1929

Martey, E., Etwire, P. M., Mockshell, J., Armah, R., & Akorsikumah, E. (2023). Ecological shocks and children's school attendance and farm work in Ghana. *World Development Perspectives, 31*, 100529.

Martinez-Taboada, C., Mera, M. J., Amutio Careaga, A., Castañeda, X., Felt, E., & Nicolae, G. (2018). The impact of cultural dissonance and acculturation orientations on immigrant students' academic performance. *Universitas Psychologica, 16*(5), 1–14. https://doi.org/10.11144/javeriana.upsy16-5.icda

McAllister, J. (2019). Esports programs don't need to break the budget to thrive. *EdTech Magazine.* https://edtechmagazine.com/higher/article/2019/12/esports-programs-dont-need-break-budget-thrive

McVilly, K., Ainsworth, S., Graham, L., Harrison, M., Sojo, V., Spivakovsky, C., Gale, L., Genat, A., & Zirnsak, T. (2022). *Outcomes associated with 'inclusive', 'segregated' and 'integrated' settings: Accommodation and community living, employment and education.* A research report commissioned by the Royal Commission into Violence, Abuse, Neglect and Exploitation of People with Disability. University of Melbourne.

Mezzanotte, C. (2022). The social and economic rationale of inclusive education: An overview of the outcomes in education for diverse groups of students. *OECD Education Working Papers, 263*, 1–93.

Michael, C. (2022, May 25). Team spirit shock the world, beat PSG.LGD to win the international 10. *Dot Esports.* https://dotesports.com/dota-2/news/team-spirit-shock-the-world-beat-psg-lgd-to-win-the-international-10

Miller, M. (2021). Video games and indirect learning: A study of 12 games that can teach. In M. Harvey & R. Marlatt (Eds.), *Esports research and its integration in education* (pp. 69–84). IGI Global.

Millipede. (n.d.). Motu Ta'e'iloa (Our Special Island). https://millipede.com.au/work/our-special-island.html

Mokobane, M., Pillay, B. J., & Meyer, A. (2019). Fine motor deficits and attention deficit hyperactivity disorder in primary school children. *South African Journal of Psychiatry*, 25.

Morgenroth, T., Stratemeyer, M., & Paaßen, B. (2020). The gendered nature and malleability of gamer stereotypes. *Cyberpsychology, Behavior, and Social Networking*, 23(8), 557–561. https://doi.org/10.1089/cyber.2019.0577

National Basketball Association. (2024). NBA 2K League. https://2kleague.nba.com

Nedera, S. (2023, May 27). *What is intersectionality? And why is it important for gender equality?* United Nations Development Programme Bosina and Herzegovina. https://www.undp.org/bosnia-herzegovina/blog/what-intersectionality-and-why-it-important-gender-equality

Newzoo. (2024). Games market trends to watch in 2024. https://newzoo.com/resources/trend-reports/games-market-trends-to-watch-in-2024

Oddone, K., Hughes, H., & Lupton, M. (2019). Teachers as connected professionals: A model to support professional learning through personal learning networks. *International Review of Research in Open and Distance Learning*, 20(3), 102–120.

Organisation for Economic Co-operation and Development [OECD]. (2019). Chapter 9. Sense of belonging at school. In *OECD, PISA 2018 results (Volume III): What school life means for students' lives*. OECD Publishing. https://doi.org/10.1787/acd78851-en

Orhan, G., & Beyhan, Ö. (2020). Teachers' perceptions and teaching experiences on distance education through synchronous video conferencing during Covid-19 pandemic. *Social Sciences and Education Research Review*, 7(1), 8–44.

Paaßen, B., Morgenroth, T., & Stratemeyer, M. (2016). What is a true gamer? The male gamer stereotype and the marginalization of women in video game culture. *Sex Roles*, 76(7–8), 421–435. https://doi.org/10.1007/s11199-016-0678

Paget, M. (2013). Cyber-bullying and the law: What should school leaders know? *Education World*. https://www.educationworld.com/a_admin/cyber-bullying-legal-issues-liability-schools.shtml

Palma-Ruiz, J. M., Torres-Toukoumidis, A., González-Moreno, S. E., & Valles-Baca, H. G. (2022). An overview of the gaming industry across nations: Using analytics with power BI to forecast and identify key influencers. *Heliyon, 8*(e08959), 2–10.

Pan European Game Information. (n.d.). What do the labels mean? https://pegi.info/what-do-the-labels-mean

Perkins, A., Clarke, J., Smith, A., Oberklaid, F., & Darling, S. (2021). Barriers and enablers faced by regional and rural schools in supporting student mental health: A mixed-methods systematic review. *Australian Journal of Rural Health, 29*(6), 835–849.

Petrova, J. (2023). *The many strengths of dyslexics*. Dyslexia Help at the University of Michigan. https://dyslexiahelp.umich.edu/dyslexics/learn-about-dyslexia/what-is-dyslexia/the-many-strengths-of-dyslexics

PewDiePie. (2024). PewDiePie [YouTube channel]. https://www.youtube.com/PewDiePie

Pfahl, L., & Powell, J. J. (2011). Legitimating school segregation. The special education profession and the discourse of learning disability in Germany. *Disability & Society, 26*(4), 449–462.

Premier League. (2023). ePremier League. https://e.premierleague.com

Preston, J. P., Jakubiec, B. A., & Kooymans, R. (2013). Common challenges faced by rural principals: A review of the literature. *Rural Educator, 35*(1), 1.

Pripas-Kapit, S. (2020). Historicizing Jim Sinclair's "don't mourn for us": A cultural and intellectual history of neurodiversity's first manifesto. In S. K. Kapp (Ed.), *Autistic community and the neurodiversity movement: Stories from the frontline* (pp. 23–39). Palgrave Macmillian.

Rashid, T., Louden, R., Wright, L., Chu, R., Maharaj, A., Hakim, I., Uy, D., & Kidd, B. (2017). Flourish: A strengths-based approach to building student resilience. In C. Proctor (Ed.), *Positive psychology interventions in practice* (pp. 29–45). Springer International Publishing.

Ready Esports. (2024a, February 17). How expensive is it to play esports: Part 1. https://readyesports.com/how-expensive-is-it-to-play-esports-part-1

References 163

Ready Esports. (2024b, February 17). How expensive is it to play esports: Part 2. https://readyesports.com/how-expensive-is-it-to-play-esports-part-2

Reframing Autism. (2023, August 14). Understanding autism. https://reframingautism.org.au/about-autism

Reitman, J. G., Cho, A., & Steinkuehler, C. (2018). *The rise of high school esports: A landscape analysis of US programs* [Report]. Connected Learning Lab. https://connectedlearning.uci.edu/wp-content/uploads/2022/09/A-Landscape-Analysis-of-High-School-Esports-in-the-United-States.pdf

Reza, A., Chu, S., Nedd, A., & Gardner, D. (2022). Having skin in the game: How players purchase representation in games. *Convergence, 28*(6), 1621–1642. https://doi.org/10.1177/13548565221099713

Ringenberg, T. R., Seigfried-Spellar, K. C., Rayz, J. M., & Rogers, M. K. (2022). A scoping review of child grooming strategies: Pre- and post-internet. *Child Abuse & Neglect, 123*, 105392. https://doi.org/10.1016/j.chiabu.2021.105392

Ringland, K. E. (2019, March 31–April 3). "Autsome": Fostering an autistic identity in an online Minecraft community for youth with autism. In *Information in contemporary society: 14th international conference, iConference 2019, Washington, DC, US, Proceedings* (pp. 132–143). Springer International Publishing.

Ripetta, S., & Silvestri, A. (2024). Exploring the embodied experience of disabilities in esports: A study on first person shooters. *puntOorg International Journal, 9*(1), 80–103.

Rogers, K. (n.d.). Autcraft: A safe haven in the gaming universe. *Abilities*. https://www.abilities.com/community/autcraft.html

Rose, A. (2023, July 23). Inside the world of female esports: "It's a scary space for women". *The Athletic*. https://theathletic.com/4635621/2023/07/23/inside-the-world-of-female-esports

Rosen, T. E., Mazefsky, C. A., Vasa, R. A., & Lerner, M. D. (2018). Co-occurring psychiatric conditions in autism spectrum disorder. *International Review of Psychiatry, 30*(1), 40–61. https://doi.org/10.1080/09540261.2018.1450229

Rosqvist, H. B., Chown, N., & Stenning, A. (Eds.). (2020). *Neurodiversity studies: A new critical paradigm*. Routledge.

Sandholtz, J. H., & Reilly, B. (2004). Teachers, not technicians: Rethinking technical expectations for teachers. *Teachers College Record, 106*(3), 487–512.

Shen, C., Ratan, R., Cai, H. C. D., & Leavitt, A. (2016). Do men advance faster than women? Debunking the gender performance gap in two massively multiplayer online games. *Journal of Computer-Mediated Communication, 21*(4), 312–329. https://doi.org/10.1111/jcc4.12159

SimStaff. (2022). The costs of hosting an esports event in 2022. https://simstaff.net/the-costs-of-hosting-an-esports-event-in-2022

Singer, J. (n.d.). Neurodiversity: Definition and discussion. *Reflections on Neurodiversity.* https://neurodiversity2.blogspot.com/p/what.html

Slee, R. (2019). Belonging in an age of exclusion. *International Journal of Inclusive Education, 23*(9), 909–922.

Smith, D. (2023a, July 10). Changing the landscape: The future of games and First Nations storytelling. *Kotaku Australia.* https://www.kotaku.com.au/2023/07/changing-the-landscape-the-future-of-games-and-first-nations-storytelling

Smith, J. C. (2023b). Esports: The need for more research to reducing neck and back pain? *Physiotherapy & Sports Injury, 1*(1), 1–2.

Smith, M. (2023c, February 3). What is mouse DPI and why does it matter for gaming? *IGN.* https://www.ign.com/articles/mouse-dpi-meaning-guide

Spielberger, C. D. (2004). *Encyclopedia of applied psychology.* Elsevier.

Standen, P. J., Camm, C., Battersby, S., Brown, D. J., & Harrison, M. (2011). An evaluation of the Wii Nunchuk as an alternative assistive device for people with intellectual and physical disabilities using switch controlled software. *Computers & Education, 56*(1), 2–10.

Statista. (2023). *Revenue of the global esports market 2020–2025.* https://www.statista.com/statistics/490522/global-esports-market-revenue

Statistia Research Department. (2024, January 26). *Cinema industry revenue worldwide from 2017 to 2026.* Statistia. https://www.statista.com/statistics/288833/cinema-industry-revenue-worldwide

Story, T., Powell, R. B., Baldwin, E., Baldwin, R. F., & Dertien, J. S. (2023). Assessing barriers to participation in environmental education field trips in the Congaree Biosphere Reserve. *Environmental Education Research*, 1–23.

References 165

Stuckey, B. (2022). About GameChanger girls. *Innovative Educational Ideas.* https://www.gamechangergirls.net/about

Sullivan, K., Perry, L. B., & McConney, A. (2013). How do school resources and academic performance differ across Australia's rural, regional and metropolitan communities? *Australian Educational Researcher, 40*(3), 353–372.

Suominen, A., Pusa, T., & Kuutti, V. (2021). Working towards gender spectrum. In N. Addison & L. Burgess (Eds.), *Debates in art and design education* (pp. 141–155). Routledge/Taylor & Francis Group.

Sweetser, P., Johnson, D., Ozdowska, A., & Wyeth, P. (2012). Active versus passive screen time for young children. *Australasian Journal of Early Childhood, 37*(4), 94–98. https://doi.org/10.1177/183693911203700413

Syahrivar, J., Chairy, C., Juwono, I. D., & Gyulavári, T. (2022). Pay to play in freemium mobile games: A compensatory mechanism. *International Journal of Retail & Distribution Management, 50*(1), 117–134.

Thomm, E., Sälzer, C., Prenzel, M., & Bauer, J. (2021). Predictors of teachers' appreciation of evidence-based practice and educational research findings. *Zeitschrift für Pädagogische Psychologie, 35*(2), 173–184.

Thorbecke, C. (2017, May 20). Single father creates a safe haven for children with autism to play together online. *ABC News.* https://abcnews.go.com/Lifestyle/single-father-creates-safe-haven-children-autism-play/story?id=47470445

Torok, L., Pelegrino, M., Lessa, J., Trevisan, D. G., Vasconcelos, C. N., Clua, E., & Montenegro, A. (2015). Evaluating and customizing user interaction in an adaptive game controller. In *Design, user experience, and usability: Interactive experience design: 4th international conference proceedings* (pp. 315–326). Springer International Publishing.

Trotter, M. G., Coulter, T. J., Davis, P. A., Poulus, D. R., & Polman, R. (2022). Examining the impact of school esports program participation on student health and psychological development. *Frontiers in Psychology, 12,* 807341.

Tuting, K. (2023, December 19). The best camera for streaming in 2023—Webcams for going live on Twitch, YouTube. *OneEsports.* https://www.oneesports.gg/gaming/best-camera-for-streaming-2023-live

Twenge, J., & Farley, E. (2020). Not all screen time is created equal: Associations with mental health vary by age and gender. *Social Psychiatry and*

*Psychiatric Epidemiology, 56*(2), 207–217. https://doi.org/10.1007/s00127-020-01906-9

United Nations. (2006). Convention on the rights of persons with disabilities. *Treaty Series, 2515*, 3.

United Nations Educational, Scientific and Cultural Organization [UNESCO]. (2023). *Global education monitoring report 2023: Technology in education—A tool on whose terms?* https://doi.org/10.54676/UZQV8501

VanDaalen, R. A., Dillon, F. R., Santos, C. E., & Capielo Rosario, C. (2024). Development and initial validation of the autism and neurodiversity attitudes scale. *Autism in Adulthood.* http://doi.org/10.1089/aut.2023.0090

Walker, I. (2020). Over 50 sexual misconduct allegations have the Super Smash Bros. community in turmoil. *Kotaku.* https://kotaku.com/over-50-sexual-misconduct-allegations-have-the-super-sm-1844328719

Warschauer, M., & Matuchniak, T. (2010). New technology and digital worlds: Analyzing evidence of equity in access, use, and outcomes. *Review of Research in Education, 34*(1), 179–225.

Wearing, J. (2022). *Online toxicity as violence in esports: A league of legends case study.* Doctoral Dissertation, Macquarie University. https://doi.org/10.25949/21499239.v1

White, T. (2020, August 13). Esports in education 101 with Jon Pratchett [Video]. Stream Semester. https://www.youtube.com/watch?v=2MFGTU9o56w

Whitlock, A., Fulton, K., Lai, M., Pellicano, E., & Mandy, W. (2020). Recognition of girls on the autism spectrum by primary school educators: An experimental study. *Autism Research, 13*(8), 1358–1372. https://doi.org/10.1002/aur.2316

Willis, P., Bland, R., Manka, L., & Craft, C. (2012). The ABC of peer mentoring—What secondary students have to say about cross-age peer mentoring in a regional Australian school. *Educational Research and Evaluation, 18*(2), 173–185.

Yao, S. X., Ewoldsen, D. R., Ellithorpe, M. E., Van Der Heide, B., & Rhodes, N. (2022). Gamer girl vs. girl gamer: Stereotypical gamer traits increase men's play intention. *Computers in Human Behavior, 131*, 107217. https://doi.org/10.1016/j.chb.2022.107217

Yao, S. X., & Rhodes, N. (2021, May). *Perceived competence (but not sexiness) drives purchase intent for video games with female leading characters* [Paper presentation, virtually]. 2021 Convention of the International Communication Association.

Yue, Y. (2017). The impact of positive school experiences and school SES on depressive symptoms in Chinese children: A multilevel investigation. *International Journal of Child, Youth and Family Studies, 8*(2), 37–58.

Zhong, Y., Guo, K., Su, J., & Chu, S. K. (2022). The impact of esports participation on the development of 21st Century skills in youth: A systematic review. *Computers & Education, 191*, 104640. https://doi.org/10.1016/j.compedu.2022.104640

# INDEX

AbleGamers, 84
Aboriginal and Torres Strait
  Islander people, 95
Acceptance, 33
Accessibility, 31–32
Accommodations as universal
  human rights, 82
Active screen time, 132
Adapting, 33
Adaptive controllers, 84–85
Adjustable furniture, 87–88
Amaze, 72
Animal Crossing, 52–53
*Animal Crossing: New Horizons*,
  60, 94–95
Artificial intelligence (AI),
  114
Atari 2600, 1
Attention deficit hyperactivity
  disorder (ADHD), 10–11,
  20, 65, 67–68
Australia, 8, 24, 95
Australian Open, 1–2
*Autcraft*, 5–6
Autism, 65–67
Autistic identity, 130
Autonomy, 32

Belonging, 30–31
'Big Mac' buttons, 89
Body-sensitive pads, 84–85
*Broken Roads*, 96
Bullying in schools, 24–25

Case study, 7–8, 44, 47, 72, 75,
  88–89, 100, 104, 117, 119
'Casual' games/gamers, 3

Cheat code, 2, 7, 15, 66, 81–82,
  110
Children's psychosocial well-being,
  129
*Chivalry* 2, 94
Cisco WebEx, 114
*Civilisation* 6, 85
Cloud gaming, 1–2
Clover Studios, 99
Clumsy child syndrome, 81–82
Cognitive development, 25–26
Collaborative teamwork, 8–9, 73
Collegiate esports, risks and
  rewards of, 131
Colonisation, 95–96
Columbine High School shooting,
  125
Communication, 93
  cards, 73–74
Community, 93, 96, 98
  mentoring within, 112–114
  of practice, 115
Community Hub, 111–112
Competition, 44
Competitive gaming, 2–3, 54–55,
  111
Competitive video gaming, 1–2
Console games, 3
Constructive communication, 9
Conventional controllers, 2–3
Cosy gaming, 52–53
*Counter-Strike:Global Offensive
  (CS:GO)* circuit, 58
COVID-19, 6–7, 26, 52–53, 59,
  114, 123
Creation of communities, 28–29

169

# Index

Creativity, 13–14, 67–68
Cultural assimilation, 26
Cultural disconnect, 26–27
Cultural dissonance, 26
Cultural diversity in semi-virtual teams, 100
Cultural understanding, 93

Dan, 12–13
*Dark Souls*, 11
Decolonisation, 22
Digital Australia, 3
Direct messages (DMs), 13
Disability, 21–22, 79
Discord, 114
Diversity and inclusivity, 5
*Doom*, 123
*Dota*2, 4, 95
Dots per linear inc (DPI), 83
DragonBear Studios, 95–96
Drop Bear Bytes, 96
Dysgraphia, 68–69
Dyslexia, 65, 68
Dyspraxia of childhood, 81–82

Economic disadvantage, 19
Economic inequality in Esports, 38–44
    avoiding microtransaction madness, 39–40
    big gaming rigs with big price points, 41
    broadcasting and video-editing hardware and software, 40
    competition and travel, 44
    costs, 39–40
    managing cost of staffing and ongoing professional development, 42–43
    physical esports spaces on budget, 43
    purchasing games, 39
Educators, 146–147
English Premier League, 1–2
Esports, 1–2, 6, 8–9, 37, 51, 93
    adapting frameworks to esports communities, 33
    challenges of economic inequality in, 38–44
    controversy, 5
    framework for inclusion in, 27–33
    Mushroom Kingdom High School, 44–47
    program, 7–8
    recommendations, 61
    researching, 9–13
    socio-economic disadvantage in esports program, 47
    tournaments, 2–3
Ethnicity and cultural background, 22
Eurocentric bias, 22
*Everyone Can Play* framework, 80
*Everyone Can Play Inclusive Esports Framework*, 17, 33–34, 36
Experience points (XP), 123

F1 Esports Series, 58
Familiarity, 84–85
*Farming Simulator*, 46
Female gamers
    challenging stereotypes of, 54–56
    current challenges, 56–57
    systems of support empowering, 57–58
Female-identifying players, 56
Fête 1 tournaments, 5
Fête 2 tournaments, 5
*FIFA/EA FC*, 13
Final Cut Pro, 40
Fine motor skills, 81
First Nations cultures, 93
Foot pedals, 84–85

Index     171

*Fortnite*, 145–146
Foundational knowledge of
    esports, 42
Framework, 27–33
Freemium games, 1–2
'From little things big things grow',
    115–116
FUSE Cup, The, 8, 59

Game development, 3
GameChanger Girls, 7–8
Gameplan, 115
Gamer girl, 57
Games, 93
Gaming, 1, 6, 51, 58, 65, 79,
    93
    colonisation, 95–96
    communities as spaces for
        neurodivergent players,
        69–72
    historical representations of
        females in, 53–54
    as transcultural phenomenon,
        94–95
Gender, 51–58
    diversity, 74
    gender-based toxicity, 51
    identity, 19–20
Geographical isolation, strategies
    to minimise, 111–117
#GGFORALL initiative, 58–59
Girl gamer, 57
Google, 1–2
*Gran Turismo* 7, 39, 141
*Grand Theft Auto*, 123–124
Gross and fine motor needs,
    81–82
Gross motor skills, 81

Health points (HP), 123
Healthy video gaming, 72
*Hearthstone*, 144
Height-adjustable desks, 87
High School Esports League, 146
*Hyper* magazine, 10
Hyrule College, 59–61

Identity, 18–24
Inclusion, 17–18
    adapting frameworks to esports
        communities, 33
    challenges, 24–27
    different levels, 27–29
    framework for inclusion in
        esports, 27–33
    keys to, 29–33
    labels of identity and differing
        priorities, 18–24
Inclusion, 82–83
Inclusive education, 22
Inclusive esports program
    educators, 146–147
    games, 133–146
    school esports, 125–132
    systems, 133
Indigenous, 23
*INDIGINERD*, 97–98
Individual needs, 28
Individualised support, 28
*Innchanted*, 95–96
Interaction, 31
Intersectionality within school
    communities, 23
Intimidation factor, 85
Involvement, 32–33

Jess, 109
*Just Dance* series, 46, 81, 137

Labels of identity, 18–24
*Last of Us Part II, The*, 54
*League of Legends*, 2–3, 39–40, 69,
    83, 100, 129, 142
*Legend of Zelda: Ocarina of Time,*
    *The*, 53
*Legend of Zelda: Twilight Princess,*
    *The*, 86–87
Level 1–1, 28
Level B, 28
Level C, 28
Level D, 28–29
Level playing field, 116
Levels, 27–29

Life skills, 9
Loneliness, 25–26

M5 World Championship, 2–3
Making decisions, 32
Marginalisation, 109
Mario, 13
*Mario Kart 8 Deluxe*, 46, 138
*Mass Effect Legendary Edition*, 54
Massively multiplayer online games
    (MMO games), 55
Matt, 11–12
Meaning context, 31
#MeToo movement, 17–18
*Metroid* series, 53–54
Metropolitan areas, 110
*Minecraft*, 5–8, 60, 88–89, 139
*Minecraft Education Edition*,
    88–89
Minor neurological dysfunction,
    81–82
Motion controls, 86–87
*Motu Ta'e'iloa*, 97
Mouse and keyboard selection,
    83–84
Multi-tiered systems of support
    (MTSS), 23–24
Multicultural esports team study,
    100
Multiculturalism
    and cultural issues in online
        gaming communities, 98
    recommendations for celebrating
        multiculturalism through
        esports, 104
Multiplayer online battle arena
    (MOBA), 9
Mushroom Kingdom High School,
    44–47

Neurodivergent players, 65
    challenges experienced in
        gaming communities, 70–72
    gaming communities as spaces
        for, 69–72
Neurodivergent students, 20, 65

Neurodivergent-inclusive esports
    program, 75
Neurodiversity, 20, 65–66, 69
    ADHD, 67–68
    autism, 66–67
    conditions, 68–69
    dyslexia, 68
Neurological conditions, 65
Neurological differences, 20
New Zealand, 7–8
Next Level Collaboration Gaming
    Group, 72, 75
Nintendo Entertainment System, 1,
    11
Nintendo Tournament Guidelines,
    133
Nintendo Wii U gamepad, 86
Non-male players, 51

OBS Studio, 40
*Ocarina of Time*, 53
Occupational skills, 9
Occupational therapists (OTs), 87
*&Omacr;kami*, 99
*Omerta*, 98
Online community users, 71
Online play, 94
Online professional learning, 115
Online toxicity as violence in
    esports, 129
Open literacy, 79
Organisation for Economic
    Co-operation and
    Development (OECD), 7
*Overwatch* 2, 39–40, 46, 140

*Pac-Man*, 1, 5
Pallet Town Primary, 100–104
Participation, 12
Participation Model, 29–30
Passive screen time, 132
PC, 41, 83
Peer–peer relationships, 131
Physical abilities, 80–88
Physical accessibility, 31
Physical disability, 81

Physical esports spaces on budget, 43
Physical needs, 79, 89
Play as force for cultural understanding and harmony, 99–100
Play games, 83–87
adaptive controllers, 84–85
adjustable furniture, 87–88
harnessing affordances of touchscreens, 85–86
motion controls, 86–87
mouse and keyboard selection, 83–84
PlayStation 5, 41
Player agency, 82–83
Player voice, 82–83
PlayStation, 10–11
PlayStation 2 (PS2), 10
Pokémon Series, 136
Power Gloves, 2–3
Problem-solving skills, 38–39
Professional associations, 42–43
Professional development for educators, 43
Professional sports organisations, 1–2

Queer, 18

Race, 22
Radicalisation through toxic gaming communities, 98–99
*Rainbow Six* series, 46
'Real' Gamer, 3
Real-time strategy (RTS), 9
Reddit, 99
Regional areas, 110
Regional esports programs, 119
Remote areas, 110
Remote esports programs, 119
Research power-up, 9, 16, 24, 128
Researching esports, 9–13
gaming for connection, 11–12
gaming for engagement, 12–13

special interest to professional pathway, 10–11
*Resident Evil*, 13
*Rocket League*, 46, 135–136
Rural areas, 110
Rural esports programs, 119

Safe spaces, 5–6
Salamanca Statement 1994, 22
Sandover Special Development School (SDS), 88–89
School communities, 6–9
School context, 20
School esports, 125–132
in Australia, 7–8
programs, 80
screen time, 132
social isolation and gaming, 129–130
violence in games, 125–128
School systems, 6–9
esports, 8–9
school esports in Australia, 7–8
Science, technology, engineering and mathematics (STEM), 7–8
Screen time, 132
Sega Master System, 11
Self-regulation, 67
Sense of belonging, 7
Side Quest, 6, 16, 96
Sims, The, 52–53
Smartphones, 1–2
Smash Sisters, 5
Social activity, 13
Social dynamics, 18
Social inclusion, 20
shifting conversation to, 23–24
Social isolation, 25–26
and gaming, 129–130
Socio-communicative interaction, 31
Socio-economic disadvantage in esports program, 47
Socio-economic status, 19

*Starcraft*, 83
*Stardew Valley*, 52–53
*Story of the Old Man Who Made Withered Trees to Flower, The*, 99
Storytelling, 95
Strategic thinking, 38–39
Streaming platforms, 114
*Street Fighter IV*, 86
Student involvement, 32–33
*Super Mario Bros*, 53
*Super Smash Bros*, 5, 39, 46, 143
*Super Smash Bros. Ultimate*, 39, 46

Teacher, 12, 27
Teamwork, 38–39
Teengers/young adults, 3
Telecommunications infrastructure, 116
Tilting monitors, 87
Touchscreens, harnessing affordances of, 85–86
Tourette's syndrome, 20
Tournament fees, 44
Travel, 44
Trolls, 6
Twitch, 1–2
21st century skills, 9

United Nations Convention on the Rights of Persons with Disabilities, 22
United States (US) National Basketball Association, 1–2
*NBA 2K* games, 1–2
2K, 2
Universal support, 28
*Untitled Goose Game*, 46
Upskilling school technicians, 42

*Valorant*, 46
Video games, 3, 53
demographics, 52–53
Video gaming, 129
Violence in games, 125–128
Viridian City School, 100–104

Wellness, 8–9
*Where in the world is Carmen San Diego?*, 12–13

Xbox, 10–11
Xbox Series X, 41
XSplit, 40

*YellowCraft* program, 130
YouTube, 1–2

Zebes College, 117–119
Zelda, 11–12, 53, 60

Printed in the USA
CPSIA information can be obtained
at www.ICGtesting.com
JSHW010835041224
74704JS00042B/121